WRITING FOR RESUI
A Resume Workbook

PAT BRETT
Emory University

Wadsworth Publishing Company
Belmont, California
A Division of Wadsworth, Inc.

© 1990 by Wadsworth, Inc. All rights reserved. No part of this book may be reproduced, stored in a retrieval system, or transcribed, in any form or by any means, electronic, mechanical, photocopying, recording, or otherwise, without the prior written permission of the publisher, Wadsworth Publishing Company, Belmont, California 94002, a division of Wadsworth, Inc.

Printed in the United States of America   49

1 2 3 4 5 6 7 8 9 10—94 93 92 91 90

CONTENTS

Preface v

Do You Know Yourself? 1
Exercise 1   Define personal success 3
Exercise 2   Get to know yourself 5

Dream Job 9
Exercise 3   Identify where you want to work 11
Exercise 4   Examine your personal needs and desires 13
Exercise 5   Examine your career needs and desires 15
Exercise 6   Summarize your career goals 17
Exercise 7   Understand corporate culture 19
Exercise 8   Picture your ideal job and organization 21

Resumes 23
Structure 25
The Chronological Resume 26
Questions Posed by First-Time Resume Writers 35
Exercise 9   Identify personal achievements 43
Exercise 10   Describe yourself 45
Exercise 11   Describe extracurricular activities 47
Exercise 12   Write your own campus activity descriptions 49
Exercise 13   Describe Greek life activities 51
Exercise 14   Write your own Greek life descriptions 55
Exercise 15   Write your own leisure time descriptions 57

Internships 59
Exercise 16   Describe internship accomplishments 61
Exercise 17   Describe internship skills 63
Exercise 18   Write your own internship descriptions 65

Volunteering 66
Exercise 19   Describe volunteer work 67
Exercise 20   Write your own volunteering descriptions 69
Exercise 21   Identify your transferrable skills 71

Exercise 22	Examine sample job descriptions	73
Exercise 23	Rewrite job descriptions	75
Exercise 24	Write your own job descriptions	79
Exercise 25	Identify your most frequently used skills	81

Newspaper Advertisement   82

Exercise 26	Write a mock resume	83
Exercise 27	Write your own qualifications statement	85
Exercise 28	Write the first draft of your resume	87
Exercise 29	Obtain feedback about your resume	89

Writing the Second Draft of Your Resume   92

Exercise 30	Evaluate the first draft of your resume	93
Exercise 31	Translate tasks performed into job descriptions	95
Exercise 32	Edit for stronger language usage	99
Exercise 33	Reevaluate your skills	101

Job Search Letters   103

The Marketing Letter   104

General Rules for Writing a Marketing Letter   104
Guidelines for a Marketing Letter   105
Sample Marketing Letters   106
Editing and Critiquing Marketing Letters   109

Exercises 34-41	Marketing letters	110
Exercise 42	Write your own marketing letter	118

Thank You or Follow-Up Letters   119

Guidelines for a Thank You Letter   120
Sample Thank You Letters   121
Editing and Critiquing Thank You and Follow-Up Letters   124

Exercises 43-50	Thank you letters	125
Exercise 51	Write your own thank you and follow-up letter	133

Appendix I	Action Words	135
Appendix II	Descriptive Words	136
Appendix III	Skills List	137
Appendix IV	Two-Letter State and Territory Abbreviations	138
Appendix V	Sources of Information: Careers and Job Listings	139
Appendix VI	Sample Resumes	140

PREFACE

READ THIS UNIQUE AD. Your resume should shout this message. Writing a job-winning document won't come easily. Procrastination will haunt you. You will need a large dose of self-discipline to self-evaluate and develop you clear career focus. Your resume must be an eye-catching advertisement that sells your credentials. Your objective: Land the job that's best for you. No small task!

Writing for Results: A Resume Workbook is designed for college students and recent graduates. Every sample in this book has been taken from a collection of more than 1000 student resumes and letters. All names and addresses have been fictionalized. Do not label any as perfect or most appropriate. Since we learn from our mistakes, I've deliberately included many that can be improved. Simply, there is no right way to do it. Look for outright errors or need for modification. You may like the look and content of a resume but observe that the objective is too broad or vague. You may see a cover letter as self-centered, where the author neglects to stress benefits for an employer. How would you phrase it? If you find examples that parallel you own experiences, tailor them to meet your personality and individual career needs.

Work these exercises from the beginning. Don't skip around. If the subject areas do not apply to you personally, read them through anyway. The language may trigger ideas that you can apply to your own experiences. If you follow the developmental pattern of these exercises, by the time you are ready to write the first draft of your resume, you will have recognized that in addition to jobs and internships your college, club, volunteering, and community activities can translate into accomplishments and skills sought after by employers.

Be patient and stick to it. Your resume will evolve as an efficient tool in your job search.

Good Luck.

Pat Brett

Do You Know Yourself?

PURPOSE AND SUMMARY:

To help you to inventory your natural skills and talents--to identify the *"comfort zone"* for your career lifestyle.

> You must know *WHO* you are within and *WHAT* you can provide for your future employer. The *who* you are consists of certain abilities, skills, desires, needs, ambitions and goals. The *what* you can provide consists of your marketable productivity and your ability to fulfill the needs of an employer who views you much like a commodity-- something to be studied and considered before buying.[*]

You will examine your personality traits, and personal and career needs and desires. You will come to understand that each of you views success differently, and will choose a variety of paths to reach goals. Some of you may be struggling to decide on a job or career objective. Forget the struggle for a moment and take the time to find out who you are. When you begin your job search, you want to know yourself well enough to seek and consider a position which enables you to achieve personal satisfaction and self-fulfillment.

In addition, you will evaluate your experiences in these areas:

- Academic
- Extracurricular
- Volunteer
- Employment

You will identify how learning situations and limited work experiences have provided transferrable skills which you will use throughout your professional life. You will find that the process of preparing to write your resume, in itself, will help you to get to know yourself. Your resume will become a reflection of your own uniqueness, individuality and past experiences.

---

[*] *The Employment Kit: A Practical Guide to Achieving Success in the Job Market.* Chicago, IL: The American Marketing Association, 1986. p. 1.

Resumes are written for the writer--for you. They help you sell yourself on you. They force you to focus and require you to organize and categorize. They challenge you to write concisely and think concretely. You have to frame your past experience and accomplishments in clear relationships to your goals. To define your job objective, you have to make a commitment to what you want. To know what you want, you have to know who you are.

When you catalogue your accomplishments, you will be amazed at what you know. You will begin to appreciate your possibilities. You will ask, "What if I use these talents to get more of what I want out of life? What if there really is a job out there that would be my *Lifework*, work that is part of my life, not just part of my job?"

Writing your resume will also help you to recognize areas where you need to get more training or experience. You may wish to polish your grasp of a foreign language to satisfy the needs of international businesses. You may need to expand your computer knowledge. You may want to volunteer to work at hospitals, or tutor. You may choose to become more involved in community affairs. In each of these, you will enrich your accomplishments and skills.

Remember:

- Resume writing is a process.

- Self-assessment is the first and crucial step.

When you skip self-assessment, you end up with a weak resume. The rewards for self-research are confidence, self-esteem, pride in what you have done and the ability to communicate your value to the employer. Employers who read your resume will invite you to an interview.

EXERCISE 1

Success!

PURPOSE:

To define *personal* success.

DISCUSSION:

Individuals are successful. Individuals make companies successful. Success does not exist in a vacuum. It is directly related to you, and to your unique and personal definition of success. You have structured its meaning from your own dreams, values and goals. Success, for you, depends on your own vision of life-satisfaction. Some of you will consider yourselves successful as reporters, others as engineers. Within each career field you will reach for different goals and change your definition as you move through life. You will build your career, and your life, on a series of small successes.

Let's take a look at *your* definition of success. Include your dreams, values and goals.

My personal statement for success is:

_____

_____

_____

_____

INSTRUCTIONS:

Evaluate your present-day *skills* and *accomplishments*. Use Appendices I, II and III for help, if needed.

Samples:

> As a result of my involvement with the student newspaper, I have learned to work independently and have polished my writing skills.

> As a result of my taking a course in Public Speaking, I am comfortable giving presentations in other courses and have developed my interpersonal communications skills.

As a result of my volunteering at Children's Hospital, I have a greater understanding of the value of good health and have nourished my ability to be gentle and caring.

1. As a result of my academic experience, I have _____
_____and developed
_____skills.

2. As a result of my academic curriculum, I have _____
_____and developed
_____skills.

3. As a result of my volunteering activities, I have _____
_____and polished
_____skills.

4. As a result of my student activities, I have_____
_____
_____ and enhanced _____
_____ skills.

5. As a result of my employment, I have _____
_____
and improved _____skills.

Based upon *all* of the above, describe yourself. This will become the first draft of your qualifications statement. Who are you? What is important to you? Are you good with your hands? Are you creative? Is that creativity artistic? Is it technical? Are you good with computers? What makes you special?

_____

_____

_____

EXERCISE 2

Personality Plus or Minus . . .

PURPOSE:

To do some personal research.

DISCUSSION:

Here's your chance to get to know yourself. You have had quality training in school, and some excellent leadership or work experience. Yet, you say you really don't know what you want to do. You may still be searching for an appealing job or career area. Sometimes the best way to begin is to examine the simple elements of your life. What are your daydreams? How would you use your own tools and style to make those dreams real? In what kind of a position would you be natural and at ease? You will need to do two kinds of research, personal and industry specific.

INSTRUCTIONS:

When describing *yourself*, act as if you are replying to interview questions. If you have had limited paid work experience, your academic, club, and volunteering activities have prepared you to give work-related answers. Emphasize personal, rather than technical, strengths. For example, if you say you are creative, consider stating that you brought a creative flair to a particular project. When you mention weaknesses, you should not give a confession of personal faults. Keep them generic and work related. Show how you addressed the problem and overcame it. For example, you have learned to handle time management problems, which led you to pay too much attention to detail or become impatient with slow-moving projects.

Begin your personal research by answering the following.

1. What traits would *others* praise in you?

_____

_____

2. What do *others* know about you that you do not recognize in yourself? Ask a *true* friend!

_____

_____

3. What personal traits would *they* suggest that you work on or modify?

_____

_____

4. What do *you* perceive as the strengths others see in you?

_____

_____

5. What do *you* perceive as your inner strengths--known only to you?

_____

_____

6. What do *you* perceive as your weaknesses or needs? Name three.

_____

_____

7. What courses have you enjoyed most? Why? Consider course content, rather than teaching effectiveness.

_____

_____

8. What courses have you enjoyed least? Why? Consider course content, rather than teaching effectiveness.

_____

_____

9. If these courses are not related to your major, do you think they will have an effect on your career choice? If yes, how?

_____

_____

10. What type of school projects did you like best? Why?

    _____
    _____

11. Do you prefer security and consistency, or do you want challenge and constant change? Why?

    _____
    _____

12. Describe your work style.

    _____
    _____

13. What kind of lifestyle do you want most for yourself?

    _____
    _____

14. What are your lifestyle goals?

    _____
    _____

15. What are your short-term career goals ?

    _____
    _____

16. What are you doing *now* to achieve your short-term goals?

    _____
    _____

17. What are your long-term goals ?

_____

_____

18. What are you doing *now* to achieve your long-term goals?

_____

_____

19. Give a job title for *your* ideal job. What would you like to be doing for the rest of your life? ***Don't*** link this *ideal job* to money, image, or power.

_____

_____

20. You have feedback from others and enhanced self-knowledge as a result of having completed this exercise. Does your definition of an ideal job match realistically with your personal goals? Is your dream job realistic or are you daydreaming? Based on your personality needs, describe your dream job.

_____

_____

_____

_____

_____

_____

_____

_____

Dream Job

Here is one student's list of characteristics for his *Dream Job.** After you complete Exercises 3-7, be prepared to make your own list.

Characteristics of the organization:

Integrity--no sleaze factor in company or industry
Change/innovation seen as positive
Growing business in a growing industry
Community service/involvement encouraged
Promotions based on merit, not seniority
Top management's outlook is long term
Learning environment
Negativism frowned upon
Participatory management is the norm
Pleasant working environment (people, physical structures)
HQ staff of 50-500
Willing and able to run promotions and marketing campaigns with class
Minimal bureaucracy, if any

Characteristics of the job:

Qualitative, people-oriented position
Opportunity to make significant contribution
Surrounded by "brilliant" people willing to share knowledge
Personal as well as promotional growth possible
Challenging
Project oriented
Enough $ to pay off student loans, live comfortably
Big city based, but involving a great deal of travel (particularly international)

Unacceptable characteristics:

Numbers crunching
Pure sales (telemarketing, commission work, etc.)
Be a peon lost in a great big bureaucracy

---

*Nemati, Darius. "Communication Skills" course assignment, Spring 1988. Quoted with permission.

- NOTES -

EXERCISE 3

Wish List!

PURPOSE:

To identify your *first choice* for kind and place of employment.

DISCUSSION:

Before you begin your job search, take a personal inventory. Where do you wish to work? WHERE refers to both work and home location, and to company size.

INSTRUCTIONS:

Answer YES or NO to the following. Would you like to:

_____ be self-employed?

_____ work for a large company?

_____ work for a small company?

_____ live in a large metropolitan area?

_____ work in a rural location?

_____ live in the suburbs?

_____ work in the suburbs?

_____ live in a rural area?

_____ work in a large urban area?

_____ work and live outside the U.S.?

_____ work and live near a large body of water?

work and live in:

_____ a. The Northeast   _____ d. The South

_____ b. The Midwest   _____ e. The Southwest

_____ c. The West   _____ f. The Northwest

_____ other _____

- NOTES -

EXERCISE 4

Personally, You Need . . .

PURPOSE:

To examine your personal needs and desires.

DISCUSSION:

You may *need* to remain living in a specific geographical area or move to a new one. Elderly or sick family members, a spouse's career or your own physical or mental health may affect your choice of job location. You may not be able to work on weekends, or you may be required to be at home at certain hours for any number of reasons.

INSTRUCTIONS:

Rate the following in terms of how each will affect your job search. What is most important (#1) or least important (#5) to you? Remember, the issue is *not* what you want, but what you *need or desire most*.

SCALE

MOST IMPORTANT				LEAST IMPORTANT
1	2	3	4	5

_____ to live and work near parents and family.

_____ to move to a new location.

_____ no weekend work.

_____ to continue present friendships and relationships in present location.

_____ flexible working hours.

_____ to make new friends while affiliating with a new organization.

_____ personal security.

_____ to work alone at home, with limited time spent at office.

_____ to work and remain living near college location.

_____ to help others.

_____ to continue present religious/community affiliations.

_____ low-pressure work environment.

_____ to find a job which requires few interpersonal communication skills.

_____ other. (Decribe below.)

_____
_____
_____
_____

ASSIGNMENT:

Select five of your #1 and #2 answers.

_____
_____
_____
_____
_____

Use these five to write a statement that describes your primary personal desires and needs.

_____
_____
_____
_____
_____

EXERCISE 5

Career-wise, You Need . . .

PURPOSE:

To examine your career objectives, so that you will seek a position in an environment where you can do your best work.

DISCUSSION:

Too many students move through their college years expecting to *get a job* after graduation. To them, finding a job is the inevitable result of receiving a degree. They accept the first job offer that comes along, and two years later they are job searching again. Their first career job should have been the result of *choice*, not *chance*. Take the time to interview with several potential employers in your career interest area. You will observe that although the job descriptions are similar, corporations will vary in the demands they make of your time, energy, and talents. Make some decisions before you accept a job offer. What are your career needs? What will make you say "No!" to a job offer?

INSTRUCTIONS:

Rate the following in terms of what is most important (#1) or least important (#5) to you. Remember, the issue is *not* simply what you want, but what you *need most*.

SCALE

MOST IMPORTANT   LEAST IMPORTANT

1   2   3   4   5

____ work on one project at a time until completed.

____ teamwork with others to achieve personal and company goals.

____ combine office responsibilities with some travel to customers.

____ a job with extensive traveling.

____ work full-time at corporate headquarters.

____ job security.

____ a job where there is little chance of relocation.

____ to write reports.

_____ an environment which encourages creativity.

_____ a people-business job.

_____ desire to do research.

_____ working in a loosely structured environment where guidance is available when you need it.

_____ desire to perform highly technical work.

_____ a high energy position in which I can prove that I work well under pressure.

_____ work alone, outdoors.

_____ work in teams, outdoors.

_____ work independently, with limited supervision.

_____ work on a variety of tasks, in a number of departments, within a company.

_____ a job with a high-status title.

_____ to advance in management.

_____ a job with a Fortune 500 company.

_____ work on a variety of tasks within my field.

_____ to gain experience.

_____ a high salary.

_____ hands-on learning.

_____ a job with good fringe benefits: insurance, company car, day care, etc.

_____ other. (Describe below.)

_____

_____

_____

_____

_____

EXERCISE 6

Summarize Your Career Goals

INSTRUCTIONS:

Select five of your #1 and #2 answers from Exercise 5.

_____

_____

_____

_____

Based on these five answers, write a statement that describes your job needs and desires.

_____

_____

ASSIGNMENT:

Combine and *edit* your personal (Exercise 4) and job desires and needs statements. In the space below, write a summary that describes your career interests and goals.

_____

_____

_____

_____

_____

_____

- NOTES -

EXERCISE 7

Corporations Have Cultures, Too . . .

PURPOSE:

To recognize that companies, like individuals, have adopted attitudes, policies and goals that make them unique.

DISCUSSION:

Webster describes culture as "development, improvement of the mind, emotions, manners, tastes, etc. . . . the ideas, customs, skills, arts, institutions of a given people in a given period; civilization."* We are used to labeling others in terms of their *culture.* We speak of the Native American culture, the Southern Culture, the Afro-American culture, the Irish or German cultures and, in fact, a culture for every segment of society--the culture of the ghetto or the culture of the mountains. Corporations, large and small, also exhibit behavioral patterns. For example, some encourage authoritarian leadership, others practice a laissez-faire management style. When you seek a career position, you are smart to research the *corporate culture.* The job itself may be ideal for you, but you may or may not be comfortable in a specific corporate environment. When you go for an office interview, absorb the subtleties of the work environment. Did you enjoy being there? Why?

INSTRUCTIONS:

Rate the following in terms of your likes (#1) and dislikes (#5).

```
                        SCALE

    LIKE                                          DISLIKE

    1           2           3           4           5
```

_2_ work in a highly structured environment with tight control.

_5_ work in teams.

_4_ work in an environment where you are left alone to get your assigned work completed.

---

* *Webster's New World Dictionary of the American Language*, Second College Edition. Englewood Cliffs, NJ: Prentice-Hall, 1986. p. 345.

_2_ work in an environment where most information is distributed through memos.

_5_ a leadership that knows how to listen as well as lead.

_4_ work under time constraints to meet deadlines.

_5_ work in a modular office setting.

_5_ work with a manager who has an "open door" policy.

_5_ wearing high-status clothing to conform to strict "dress" policy.

_4_ work for a company where you are relatively sure of long-time employment. (The company assumes a paternal role.)

_5_ work with a manager who gives frequent feedback.

_4_ work for a corporation that addresses the need for high personal and corporate ethical standards.

____ work in a no-nonsense, shirt-sleeves environment.

_5_ work under project or task orientation.

_5_ work within a company where employees are involved in decision making.

_3_ work within a company where there are regularly scheduled meetings (e.g., every Monday or Friday).

_5_ having a say in corporate objectives.

_5_ work within an environment that promotes and rewards ability rather than seniority.

_3_ work within an environment that promotes and rewards seniority, while recognizing that an employee has achieved seniority because of proven ability.

____ other. (Describe below.)

_____

_____

INSTRUCTIONS: List your #1 and #2 answers.

work in highly structured - tight control environment uses memos.

_____

EXERCISE 8

Picture Your Ideal Job and Organization

INSTRUCTIONS:

List the characteristics of your Dream Job and Organization. At the end, add what you do not want to do. Select from your #1 and #2 answers in Exercises 4-7. After you have completed the list, be prepared to select from the list and write a complete-sentence, full-paragraph statement which *describes* the job and the organization that are most appealing to you.

Characteristics of the Organization:
- A progressive/innovative company
- Company with long term objectives
- Open concept with little departmental barriers

Characteristics of the Job:
- Project oriented
- Responsibility driven
- Descision making

Least Acceptable Characteristics:
- Superiors who look for short term-base descisions
- No investment into company

Read all you can about Corporate Culture, and consult with the counselors at your Career Counseling Center. In what kind of an organization do you hope to work? Look back at all of your #5 answers in Exercises 4-7. These are the negatives. Keep them in mind.

- NOTES -

Resumes

PURPOSE AND SUMMARY:

Your resume is the passport to the interview, your first impression, the most important document in your job search. An effective resume speaks for you and reveals who you are and how you can benefit an employer. "It is a condensed, efficient description of you."[*] It can open doors to a successful career. A limp resume, void of personality, can eliminate you. Be prepared to call attention to your accomplishments and their results. Your resume should contain far more than a listing of courses taken and tasks performed. It is not your autobiography; it is a written advertisement. Here are five rules for resume writing:

Be Brief!

Keep your resume to one page, if possible. Additional pages reduce your chances for securing an interview. A large advertisement in a national newspaper can bring 1000 replies in a few days. The first reading of these resumes, a skimming only, is given 30-45 seconds, at most. A well-written one-page resume, with quantified details, tells the reader that you have strong planning and organizational skills. Communicate for results. Orient your job descriptions toward a specific job goal. A busy evaluator does not have the time to wade through a long resume, overloaded with facts and too light on achievements. The process of evaluation is really a process of elimination. Job candidates selected for interviews have succinct resumes. Make it easy for an evaluator to identify your skills, accomplishments, communication strengths and similar previous skills experiences.

Be Honest!

Do you know that there are national credential verification services? They work with companies to check the specifics on your resume. The more responsible the job, the more they check. Even if you can prove that you attended five years of college, don't claim to have earned a degree if you don't have one. If you have interned for six months at a large company, don't represent it as a full-time job. Be honest! Don't lie! Managers are wary of the accomplishment section. It is where most of the "creative writing" takes place. Make sure yours is true and realistic. Bluffing and exaggeration are dumb. On the other hand, remember that a potential employer should receive only positive information. You have no obligation to share personal facts or information which will hurt you. As long as you present yourself honestly, past negatives have no business on a resume. Employers prefer to have candidates who appear to be winners.

---

[*] Timm, Paul R., and Jones, Christopher G. *Business Communication Getting Results*, 2nd edition. Englewood Cliffs, NJ: Prentice-Hall, 1987. p. 369.

Rewrite!

Don't be afraid to work up two or even three resume drafts until you're completely satisfied with the end result. The exercises in this workbook will trigger your thinking and give you samples of how others formatted resumes, wrote experience descriptions, measured their accomplishments and identified their skills. Employers have been known to grant interviews because they wanted to meet people who cared so much about themselves and their careers that they prepared and submitted first-class resumes.*

Use Eye Appeal!

Grab the attention of the reader. Present a professional, typed resume, free of errors. If possible, use a computer and a laser printer. Information stored on a disk can be updated, revised and polished until it meets quality standards. You can correct misspellings, alter the layout and have the advantage of using a choice of lettering and type sizes. Leave wide margins and plenty of white space. Do not include a photograph unless your appearance is crucial to the job. All of the sample resumes in this workbook have been generated on computers. Look at them from an *eye appeal* point of view. Which ones do you like? Why? As long as all of the necessary information is on your resume, you have the option to choose your own style. Perhaps you would like to mix some of the techniques. Why not? *Your* resume should reflect *your* personality. When you are satisfied with both content and *look*, print your finished copies on 100% rag paper. This paper feels finer, richer and more professional. Choose a conservative color. White is always acceptable. If you select an off-white or ivory, be sure it is a subtle tan, not brown. Avoid pastel colors and gray which looks like silver. Recruiters find it easier to read a resume printed on off-white or ivory paper.

Direct Your Resume Toward Results!

When prospective employers read your resume they should find the answer to the question, "What's in it for me?" Achieve this response through the construction of a *you*-centered resume. Here are some tips:

- Know who you are, where you want to go and how you plan to accomplish your personal goals.

- Develop your career objective.

- Make a commitment to what you want.

- Research the company--your audience.

---

* Adapted from Good, C. Edward. *Does your Resume Wear Blue Jeans?* Charlottesville, VA: Word Store, 1985. p. 7.

- Be selective! Will this company, and the specific job opportunity, satisfy your career plan?

- If you like the "match," locate a copy of *their* description of the job opening.

- Match your job objective on your resume to *their* need.

- Design your skills and accomplishment statements to support *their* job description.

- Understand that the best job match takes place when both you and the company have common values and objectives.

Structure

PURPOSE AND SUMMARY:

Choose an appropriate resume format. Savvy builders consult detailed architectural plans before attempting to construct houses. Most often, they refine the plans to design structures to match available money, space and location. They recognize that this customized plan is necessary for successful results. Resume writers need to do the same. You need to customize and structure your resume for results. Don't let it become a close copy of someone else's resume. You want to create your own style. All of the sample resumes in this book are real resumes. If you were to evaluate them, you would say that some are more focused, have greater depth or simply are more eye appealing. There is no one perfect resume. The perfect resume, for you, is the one you keep changing to upgrade your layout, language, experience, and expertise.

The Chronological Resume Format

You are about to "build your first house," to select one of the first full-time positions in your career path. Part of your consideration is form or format--where and how much information should appear on your one-page resume? Where will you place specific information to get attention and to satisfy employer needs for easy reading? The chronological resume format tells, in reverse chronological order, your responsibilities, achievements, and skills used for each position you have had. It emphasizes what you did, when you did it, and for whom you did it. It is straightforward and easily understood. Chronological resumes are most popular with college career counselors and employers who are interviewing entry-level job candidates. If you are in school or have graduated within the last two or three years, this format is probably right for you. It categorizes your life and reveals your *Education, Activities, Employment* and *Other Data* which is of special value in your job search. You highlight your honors, membership in organizations and leadership positions, as well as your employment history. It enables your employer to see your diversity and accomplishments and to make conclusions about your abilities, skills, and employment qualifications. Chronological resumes show a pattern of academic training supplemented by work experience. Frequently, volunteer and extracurricular activities make up a large segment of your experiences. It is up to you to highlight your creativity and entrepreneurial talent. All but one of the exercises and resume samples in this workbook follow the chronological format. The overwhelming majority of entry-level job candidates should use the chronological resume. Employers prefer it. A sample resume with a chronological format appears on page 32.

The Functional Resume Format

The functional resume works best for people with significant experience in a variety of fields. It can also be very effective when showing a number of experiences in a specific career area. In a functional resume, skills, rather than work experience, are your greatest selling point. Areas of achievement are highlighted in categories. The main thrust of a functional format is what you've accomplished, with less emphasis on when and for which employer. Information laid out under these main category headings describes achievements that fit those headings. The format is very results-oriented.

The functional layout also works well for career changers and re-entry workers. Most entry-level job seekers do not have enough depth of experience to use this format. A sample of a resume with a functional format appears on page 33.

The Chronological Resume

Before you begin, be sure that you have read the answers to questions commonly asked by college students on pages 35-41. Here is a flexible format for the Chronological Resume.

HEADING

Your heading contains your name, address and telephone number. Place it in the center, at the top of the page. Use a bold print for your name, and choose a print size larger than that used for your address and telephone number. Use discretion! You want to gain immediate attention, but you don't want it to be so large that it overpowers the rest of your resume. Avoid abbreviating the street and state names unless one line extends beyond the others and upsets the balance and appearance of your caption. In that case, use United States Postal Abbreviations. They appear in Appendix IV. Use the name you want to be known by in a professional business situation. Don't resort to using nicknames.

Samples:

NO:

Mark Jeffrey Holland
10 Eden Rd.
East Highland Falls, New Hampshire   03755
(603) 555-1234

YES:

Mark Jeffrey Holland
10 Eden Road
East Highland Falls, NH   03755
(603) 555-1234

If you are attending school away from home, use a two-address caption. Here are some variations of titles. You can change them to suit your taste.

Katherine Abbott Collins

School Address
Box 47927
Top University
Providence, RI 12345
(701) 555-1234

Home Address
44 Flamingo Drive
Smithtown, NY 11787
(516) 555-0920

Andrew M. Emmett

Present Address
Box 23320
Top University
Phoenix, AZ 85016
(602) 555-1234

Permanent Address
5274 Lower River Road
Lewiston, NY 14092
(716) 555-7870

Some students simply list their temporary address at the left, if it is easily identified because it contains a school name and box number. They place their permanent address at the right; they do not use a title, and center their names at the top.

Jonathan Brett Powers

Box 44760
Top University
Nashville, TN 37222
(615) 555-1234

472 Forge Road
Orlando, FL 34762
(904) 555-3257

OBJECTIVE

An objective tells the reader what job you seek. Sometimes, a short, crisp statement is appropriate, especially if it is a specific job title.

Samples:

> Entry-level position in accounting with emphasis on taxes.
>
> A position as a travel agent.
>
> A summer position in retail sales.
>
> A computer consulting internship.

For those of you seeking a full-time permanent position, expand your objective, without being wordy. Include the level of the desired position and the skills you can bring to a job. Grab the recruiter's attention. Give additional information. Add *energy* to the job title or category.

Samples:

> A position as a sales management trainee requiring marketing and organizational skills.
>
> Seeking a supervisory position in a financial institution using experience in banking and public relations.
>
> An apprentice position in the entertainment industry that will use and enhance communications skills developed through academic studies.
>
> A position in the field of corporate employee health promotion and wellness teaching.

If your resume represents a self-advertisement, *your* sales campaign should begin in your job **OBJECTIVE** where you identify how you can benefit an employer. Before writing your objective, consider your would-be employer, your audience--the one or more persons who will review your resume. What will get results? Should your objective be short and direct, more detailed or should it move into what you would label a **PROFILE** or a **QUALIFICATIONS SUMMARY**. You will write both of these on page 46 and 86, and may want to polish and tighten them up for use on your resume.

The **QUALIFICATIONS SUMMARY** or simply **SUMMARY** is especially appropriate when you want to call attention to the technical and personal skills that qualify you for a specific job. Some students include both an **OBJECTIVE** and a **SUMMARY**. The **OBJECTIVE** states the job they seek. The **SUMMARY** includes at least one accomplishment, supported with a summary of skills used. It must reinforce your employment goals, and be no more than two or three sentences long.

EDUCATION

As a student or new graduate keep this section up front; it is probably your greatest asset and accomplishment. Recruiters want to get immediate basic information about you. Name your educational institution and your specific degree first. Refer to pages 37-38 for information about including other schools, course listings, special technical training and other courses or seminars that have upgraded your skills. Give the date you received or will receive your degree, and name your major.

Consider adding your GPA. If it is 3.0 or above, include it. Recruiters seek intelligent job candidates. If your cumulative GPA is less than 3.0 but you have a 3.2 in your major, label it as such. Sometimes your GPA doesn't reflect how well you did in school. This often happens if you enrolled in rigorous college courses. You may have earned a B, but others may have grades far below yours. You may be one of the top students in a difficult program. If this is the case, you may want to consider listing your courses. Don't even mention your GPA if you feel that it hurts your job search. Ask your career counselors if employers in your field ask for GPA information. Accounting firms, for example, almost always want it to be part of your resume.

Samples:

Best College, Northampton, MA
BS in Physics. May 19XX. GPA in Major 3.32

Top University, Tucson, AZ
Candidate for BS in Nursing, May 19XX

Best College, Wheaton, IL
AA, Computer Science. 19XX

Top University, Davis, CA
BBA, Finance. May 19XX
Finance GPA: 3.74
Cumulative GPA: 3.50

Top University, New York, NY
BA with Honors in Psychology, 19XX. GPA: 3.7

HONORS AND ACTIVITIES

Add this subheading under **EDUCATION**. Here is an appropriate place to add information about your college life, which will be of value to an employer. It is where you will name any scholarships, awards, and certainly your being placed on the Merit or Dean's List.

If your activities reinforce your academic training and make you a better-prepared candidate for a specific job, be sure to include it here. Be selective. Do *not* name every activity in which you were involved. If your college activities are *not* connected to the job you seek, do a self-test. As you consider each activity, ask yourself, "Will it reveal certain abilities, attitudes, skills or talents which can be transferred to enhance my job performance or customer satisfaction?" If the answer is yes, include it; if no, leave it out. Refer to Exercises 11-14 on pages 47-55. There are times when college activities are appropriately classified under EXPERIENCE.

Samples:

Top University, Detroit, MI
Bachelor of Science in Business Administration
May 19XX. Major: Accounting. GPA: 3.47

Honors and Activities:

Dean's List
Beta Alpha Psi Fraternity, Vice President
VITA (Volunteer Income Tax Assistance) Program
Accounting Lab Instructor
University Board Travel Committee Publicity Chairman

Top University, Washington, DC
Candidate for BA degree, May 19XX
Major: Communications. GPA: 3.36

Honors and Activities:

Dean's List
Alpha Delta Pi Sorority
    Best Pledge Award
    Prize Chairman: Communicated with members of Washington's business community while seeking donations for prizes to be awarded at the Disabled Children fund raiser.
    Volunteer: Washington Area Services for the Blind

EXPERIENCE

This is the body of your resume. Your most recent position should be listed first. Give job title, dates of employment, name and location of employer. If you have held more than one title with the same employer, give your most recent title first, followed by the job description and dates you held the title. As you go back through your experiences, give additional titles and job descriptions.

Job descriptions should name your tasks, accomplishments and skills used or enhanced. As you prepare your descriptions, use a practice note page. Name the tasks and then link the tasks to what you accomplished and to the skills you used. Avoid sentences starting with *Responsible for* or *Duties included*. When you do, you may find yourself listing a series of tasks without linking them directly to accomplishments and skills. Refer to Exercise 22 on page 73.

Use verbs like *supported* or *participated* instead of *helped* or *assisted* for stronger language usage.

If room permits, place each job description on a new line. If you bullet them, they will stand out. Include numbers, percentages, and honors. Identify how you exceeded quotas or standards of excellence. Be sure to use brief statements, rather than long sentences. Avoid large blocks of information. Start each with an active verb and *do not use* personal pronouns. Refer to the samples in Exercies 16-25 on pages 61-81.

If part of your **EXPERIENCE** includes school-, volunteer-, or community-related positions of leadership, the length of your job descriptions will probably equal the rest of your strongest *paid* employment descriptions. You will use less space as you go back in time.

No need to include jobs held for very short periods, especially if they have no relation to the job you are seeking. However, even a job driving your own ice cream truck during summer vacation can tell an employer that you have entrepreneurial spirit, a commitment to daily outdoor work, and probably good communication skills. All of these characteristics will make you an asset to an employer. Don't downplay any of the typical *vacation* jobs. Many of them give you a broad view of people and companies. Sometimes they help you to clarify your career goals. After holding an internship or summer position in your career field, you may realize that you do *not* want to pursue your original career choice.

Remember, your resume should show a chronological history of working, even if it is for a three- or four-year period. Employers respect students who have worked during time off from studies.

OTHER DATA

Here is another opportunity to tailor your resume to your own needs. Develop your own strategy! If you have special skills, credentials or strong experience that needs highlighting, *create your own sub-heading*. Choose to use this format if one or more of the following categories support your specific job objectives and career goals.

- Professional Associations
- Computer Proficiencies
- Licenses or Certificates
- Community Service
- Athletics
- Languages
- Travel
- Military

If you simply want to draw attention to a number of additional accomplishments, professional interests or job qualifications, put them in one category and label it **OTHER DATA**. Many college students find that this works best for them. Be careful! Don't let this category become a catch-all. Self-search to be sure that you include information that has value for an employer. Make an employer see you as an interesting person who brings additional qualifications to a job.

Sample: Chronological Resume
STEPHEN P. REDDEN

Present Address:
1563 Ponce de Leon Ave., N.E.
Nashville, TN 30000
(609) 555-5243

Permanent Address:
4 Madison Avenue
New York, NY 12954
(212) 555-8679

OBJECTIVE A position using interest and skills in human resource management.

EDUCATION TOP UNIVERSITY, School of Business Administration, Nashville, TN
BBA with concentration in Finance and Management, May 19xx
Grade Point Average: 3.5/4.0

Coursework includes:
- Financial Accounting
- Managerial Accounting
- Real Estate
- Executive Power and Negotiations
- Personnel Administration
- Management Decision Laboratory

Mediation Training Program: Founding member
- Group of students and faculty trained to mediate conflicts in college environment.

HONORS and ACTIVITIES:
Dean's List
Alpha Epsilon Pi Fraternity
Participated in intramural team sports
Volunteer: "Much Ado About Midtown" committee

EXPERIENCE ABC Computer Corp., Central Marketing Div. Summer 19xx
Administrative Assistant New York, NY
- Summarized and arranged Employee Opinion Survey Data.
- Created Customer Orientation Presentation using "Slidewrite" software.
- Updated and maintained confidential personnel files.
- Developed a working knowledge of the Professional Office System communications network (PROFS), LOTUS 1-2-3 and Displaywrite.

ABC Computer Corp., Americas/Far East HQ Summer 19xx
Administrative Assistant New York, NY
- Served as the Business Practices' department secretary.
- Constructed a complete index of Americas/Far East contracts on an IBM PC using PFS: File and Report.
- Reviewed, revised, and corrected customer claims reports.
- Operated the 8100 DOSF Basic Operator System and PROFS.
- Responsible for handling confidential material.
- Received **special cash award** for outstanding performance.

ADDITIONAL DATA Knowledge of BASIC and FORTRAN computer languages.
Enjoy team sports, jazz music and travel.

Sample: Functional Resume
JENNIFER L. CRAWFORD

1714 Woodcliff Way
Seattle, WA 98122
(206) 555-0623

6859 Poppy Street
Pittsburgh, PA 15208
(412) 555-1748

Profile:	Creative, energetic individual with a versatile and enterprising background seeks a position in advertising.
Education:	**Top University,** Seattle, WA. May, 19xx. Bachelor of Arts, Psychology.
	Top University, Cambridge, MA. Summer studies program 19xx. Education in Psychology and Theater Studies.
Mass Communications Experience:	**Shar & Smart,** Seattle, WA, 19xx. Advertising copywriting internship. Helped produce an interoffice Monday morning memo and assisted on creative input for several accounts including Washington Power, NAPA, Cellular First, and Graphics Plus.
	Open City, Seattle, WA, 19xx. Editorial internship with Seattle-based arts and entertainment magazine; developed skills in writing, sales, and interviewing techniques.
	DEF News Seattle Bureau, Seattle, WA, 19xx. Assistant Affiliate News Producer. Retrieved information from northwest affiliates and relayed information to the broadcasting bureau in New York; selected and assisted with promotion of current events for broadcasting.
	Central News Network, Seattle, WA, 19xx. Communications internship with the Special Reports Unit; assisted Associate Producer on special report, "*A Woman's Place*"; developed editorial and technical skills.
	The Ninety's Woman, Seattle, WA, 19xx. Editorial internship with an international trade paper for the wholesale and retail fashion industry. Interviewed retailers and manufacturers, assisted with editorial fashion shoots, and wrote business features.
Sales Experience:	**Meghan's,** Cambridge, MA, 19xx. Sales associate in a unisex European clothing boutique; developed skills in promoting unique products to American culture.
	Brittany Fashions, Cambridge, MA, 19xx. Sales clerk; assisted customers in purchase selection. Recognized for outstanding services.

- NOTES -

What if Questions!!!

PURPOSE:

To answer questions posed by first-time resume writers.

I don't really know what I want to do.
Counselors at your Career Counseling Center often conduct personality and sensitivity interviewing as well as career preference inventories. This kind of self-testing should help you link your abilities and personal and professional skills to appealing opportunities in the job market.

When you go to your Career Planning and Placement Office, or to a large public library, look for books, pamphlets and articles that contain listings of sources of employment. You should also find computerized career information systems which allow for quick retrieval of data on current employment, wages and salaries, working conditions, and job outlook. Use Appendix V to find a listing of sources of information about careers, job listings and potential employers. Don't limit yourself to this list. Use it as a stepping-off point. New directories and career publications appear on the market on a regular basis. Make use of the most recent information available.

I don't know what jobs exist in my career interest area.
Look for a copy of *The Occupational Outloook Handbook."* It's compiled by the U.S. Department of Labor and is available from the U.S. Government Printing Office. Then seek out your career counselors for further information.

An expensive commercial resume writing service representative said that I should print RESUME OF QUALIFICATIONS at the top of my resume.
Why? If it isn't completely obvious from the very look of your content material, you have a problem. Others call a resume a Curriculum Vita, a Vita or a Fact Sheet. There is no reason to give a title or label to your resume. Use available space to focus attention on your strengths and show yourself as a powerhouse of an employee.

I have been given conflicting information about whether or not to include a job objective.
If you are attending or just graduating from college, you are smart to include a job objective. This is especially true for students with a Liberal Arts education. Employers don't know, from looking at your resume, what job you seek. For instance, Political Science, English or Science majors may be seeking any number of positions in many fields. If you know exactly what job you seek, be as specific as possible. You may want to tailor your objective and *create* an entire resume for a particular job. Most recruiters want entry-level job seekers to target a specific area of interest. When you say that you are seeking a position in *any* part of a company, you could be saying *nonverbally*:

- Just give me a job anywhere.
- I have not planned for a short-term goal.

You will see that the sample resumes in Appendix VI use headings labeled **OBJECTIVE, PROFILE** and/or **SUMMARY**. Choose any of these labels, and be sure that your career objective is specific or implied.

Later on, after a number of years of work experience, you may begin your resume with an Accomplishments section, a Profile or a Qualifications Summary. At that time, you can be more flexible about writing a job objective. In Exercise 27, page 85, you will be asked to focus your objective and the descriptive wording on your resume to answer a specific job advertisement.

I want to use my nickname on my resume.
Don't! Your resume is a professional document.

I am strongly involved with a political organization.
Someone somewhere said, "Never argue about politics or religion." A similar warning could apply as you begin your job search. Your religious or political affiliation is your personal business. Aside from possible discrimination, there is a fine line that you must address for yourself. How much personal information do you choose to include in a *public* document, your resume? You risk rejection if you include, in your resume, your work for or affiliation with a political or religious group. Don't get yourself screened out before you have even had a chance to interview. This information fits into the illegal question category, so you are within your rights not to include it. The same rules apply for age, race, sex and national origin. Consider also that you may not want to work for an organization where people are strongly opposed to your beliefs.

I have a B/C average and no involvement in clubs or activities. What should I do? Where should I begin?
What did you do in past jobs? Where did you excel there? Describe everything which makes you marketable. How strong is the academic program at your school? You may not have earned an "A," but your courses and the program itself may have given you depth in your field. List your courses. Did you work while attending college? Include this information on your resume. Your grades may reflect the heavy burden of performing on the job, attending class and completing your homework.

I expect to job search in another state.
If you are seeking a job outside the geographical location of your degree-granting school, and you are unsure of whether your school is well known in that location, include, on your resume, a listing of courses taken. Choose those which complement and add support to your qualifications for a specific job. People in Pennsylvania can not be expected to be familiar with every academic program in New Mexico, although they can locate that information in a number of reference books.

I have very little work experience.
College students are *not* expected to have a long employment history. Your *work* is school work. However, you may find that you have a great deal of

experience that will prove valuable to an employer. If you have been active in clubs, or fraternal, Greek, or community organizations, you may have a great deal to offer. The sample descriptions and workbook assignments also give you some good ideas. Review Exercises 11, 12, 13, and 19. They have been included in this workbook to give you examples of how students have described college and community-related activities. They will also provide direction for writing your own work descriptions.

I've attended more than one college.
If you expect to earn a degree from the college you are now attending, list your present school first. If you have a degree from another school, list that school under it.

Sample:
    Best College, Ripon, WI
    Candidate for BA in Economics, May 19XX

    Best College, Racine, WI
    AA, Liberal Arts, May 19XX

I've attended more than one college while completing my degree over a long period of time.
You have no obligation to list the names of all the schools you attended, nor do you have to explain why you did not complete your degree in a specific time period. However, you should name those schools that will show that you have depth in academic studies. If you attend a well-respected school and earned some credits in a particular field, name the school and the courses.

Sample:
    Best College, Ripon, WI
    Candidate for BA in Economics, May 19XX

    Top University, New York, NY
    Completed French literature and civilization
    courses while developing and increasing foreign
    language communication skills, fall 19XX.

I've attended another college for special studies.
Many students take special courses to enrich academic, technical, language or international experience. Some take courses while traveling. Sometimes they study for the summer, a semester or year in another location. They experience the culture, and perhaps business practices, in another environment. Place the name of that institution under the name of your degree-granting school.

    Best College, Ripon, WI
    Candidate for BA in Economics, May 19XX

    Top University, Exeter, England
    Summer Study Abroad Program, summer 19XX
    Participated in extensive sociobiological
    research on British elementary school children.

I worked my way through school.
More credit to you. Most students choose to include this information under **OTHER DATA**, although it is also appropriate in the **EDUCATION** section. Don't leave it out! Here are some examples of how students have described their work experiences.

Samples:

>Earned a substantial portion of educational expenses through summer employment and the University Work Study Program.
>
>Financed 100% of college expenses through summer and afternoon employment during school.
>
>Financed 30% of college education through part-time jobs and college loans.
>
>Have financed 100% of education through scholarships, loans and employment.

I attended college part-time while holding a full-time job.
Most employers will be delighted to have you. They recognize motivation, strong character, positive attitude, and a willingness to work hard to achieve a goal. Be sure that you include this information on your resume.

Samples:

>Earned 36 college credit hours during a two-year period, while working full-time.
>
>Worked 40 hours a week while completing requirements for BA degree.
>
>Completed courses for BS degree in six years, while holding a full-time job.

I spent four years in the military.
Often, companies in the defense sector seek out those with a good military record. Some organizations wonder if you may be too regimented. Commercial airline companies take a close look at pilots who have served in the military. A "hot shot" may risk passenger safety. Other companies consider you an asset because you will bring order to an undisciplined organization. If you choose to include your military service experience, include a section titled **MILITARY** or **MILITARY SERVICE**. Name your branch of service, highest rank, honors and awards. If you have special skills be sure to describe them, especially when they could further your civilian career. Give the date of your honorable discharge.

I speak a foreign language.
Many of you have a working, fluent, or proficient knowledge of one or more foreign languages. Include languages under **OTHER DATA**. If it is a direct requirement for the job you seek, name it in your **OBJECTIVE** or **PROFILE**. Qualify your descriptions. If you have studied a foreign language for a number of years, and could brush up on it quickly, identify yourself as having a working knowledge. If you speak a second language at home, although you have not had academic training, be sure to name it. You will be an asset to companies active in today's global market.

Samples:

> Fluent in Spanish conversation.
>
> Reading, writing and speaking proficiency in German and Russian languages.
>
> Knowledge of basic communication skills in the Japanese language.

I have computer knowledge and experience.
You have three options:

If the job you seek is directly related to computers, include a specific reference to computer skills in your **OBJECTIVE, PROFILE** or **SUMMARY**.

Refer to specific computer languages, programs, hardware and software when you write your job descriptions for positions you have held that required computer use and experience.

Place computer knowledge under **OTHER DATA** if you want the reader to know that you are generally familiar with languages, hardware and software. Here are some examples.

Samples:

> Working knowledge of BASIC computer language.
>
> Knowledge of Lotus 1-2-3, Wordstar, Apple Macintosh, and IBM computers.
>
> Knowledge of BASIC and FORTRAN computer languages and elementary programming techniques.

I started my own business.
Employers seek your entrepreneurial spirit. Creative, innovative people fit well in research and development areas. In addition, employers recognize that you have broad-based practical business experience. You have an overall perspective and it's a good bet you have strong communication skills. Here are some student examples.

Samples:

Founder and Manager
Mercury Resurfacing, New London, CT
Founded home outdoor repair company specializing in driveway resurfacing. Managed finances. Improved motivating and marketing skills. Employed three laborers. Netted more than $17,500 during a three-month period.

Self-Employed
Tom Thumb Cares, Novi, MI
Initiated and managed a child-care service. Set prices, delegated assignments to three workers, kept books and designed promotional brochures.

Look for Gary Price's resume in Appendix VI on page 154. He earned enough money to put himself through undergraduate and graduate school. He was also one of the first in his class to receive a great job offer, *before* graduating.

I don't know what to call my job. No one ever gave me a title.
Contact the company to see if your work appears under one of their occupational titles. If not, label your title by the work you did.

I was an outstanding student in high school. Should I include it on my resume?
That depends. If you have not had similar successes in college, recruiters will want to know why. If you have been an academic and student leader in college, that information should take precedence on your resume. Employers want to know what you have been doing for the last two to four years. Students who have been high school valedictorian or an Eagle Scout may consider placing these superior accomplishments on their resumes.

I'm a freshman. I don't need a resume.
Yes, you do! You never know what will come up. You may find yourself seeking a leadership position on a school organization. In a few months, you may want to present yourself as a candidate for a summer job or internship. Your resume may not be long, but it should highlight your skills and accomplishments so far. This is a time when it is appropriate to include high school activities.

I don't have any references.
Get started now! Begin to gather two forms of references.

First, comprise a list of names, titles, addresses, and phone numbers of those who know you and respect your work. Select a balance from three areas.

- Personal: Those you know personally and can vouch for your character

- Academic: Professors and advisors

- Professional: Employment supervisors and managers

Two or three from each group should be sufficient. Be sure to get permission from each person before you use his or her name. This list of references is provided to your prospective employer upon request, as indicated on your resume. Print it on a separate piece of the same quality paper and be ready to present it to a recruiter during an interview.

Sample:

REFERENCES

PERSONAL:

Dr. John O'Donnel, M.D.
1523 Midland Avenue
Bronxville, NY 10708

Ms. Dorothy Van Hall
P.O. Box 1234
Hartsdale, NY 10530

ACADEMIC:

Dr. Delores Staudt, Ph.D.
Professor of Biology
Best College
New Rochelle, NY 10805

Dr. Lee McManus, Ph.D.
Professor of Psychology
Top University
School of Medicine
Salt Lake City, UT 48115

PROFESSIONAL:

Dr. Kevin Wheatley, M.D.
Resident Director
Caring Medical Center
Salt Lake City, UT 48115

Dr. Anna V. Rogers, M.D.
Medical Director
Caring Medical Center
Salt Lake City, UT 48115

The second reference group contains a portfolio of reference letters. If possible, request these letters before you leave each job. Some of you may have copies of letters sent to support your entry-qualifications for schools or scholarships. If people think well enough of you to send a reference letter, they are usually willing to give you a copy. Keep the originals. When future employers ask for reference letters, make copies and present the letters that best support your candidacy for a job.

- NOTES -

EXERCISE 9

Create a Portfolio of Your Personal Achievements

PURPOSE:

To identify your personal accomplishments and to examine your values and motivations to succeed.

DISCUSSION:

We all remember events, accomplishments, awards and honors which have contributed to our own (sense of) self-esteem. Sometimes we gained public recognition; at other times these personal achievements seemed unimportant to others, but meant a great deal in our private lives. In this exercise, name some of the personal achievements that have meant a great deal to you. You will better understand the "inner you" when you examine your values, motives and feelings. Be ready to ask yourself *why* you label yourself successful. In some cases, it is easy to understand why you won a medal or earned a high GPA. In other cases this exercise will help you get a better understanding of your own character. You may like or dislike what you find. Use Appendices I, II and III.

INSTRUCTIONS:

A. If you were to create a portfolio of your accomplishments, what would you include? They may or may not be job or school related. Be sure to consider your *private successes* as well as *public honors*.

Samples:

- Designed and installed a home stereo system.
- Selected for intensive studies of the Spanish language at Best University, Madrid, Spain.
- Developed and conducted a mathematics tutoring program at a College Preparatory School.

List *four* of your accomplishments. Identify for yourself why *you* label them as accomplishments.

1. _____

2. _____

3. _____

4. _____

43

B. If you were to create a portfolio of what *you perceive* as your highest achievements, what would it include?

Samples:

- Counseled troubled ten-year-olds in a summer camp.
- Joined Habitat for Humanity to build homes for the poor.
- Interviewed and selected candidates for the Honor Council.
- Acted as a *Big Sister* to a high school student.
- Gave a successful presentation to a group of 100 doctors.

List *four* of your accomplishments. Identify for yourself why *you* label them as accomplishments.

1. _____
2. _____
3. _____
4. _____

C. How have you *exceeded* standards of excellence?

Samples:

- Achieved an "A" in an advanced physics course.
- Earned an engineering degree in only three years.
- Graduated in the top 10% in a class of 600 at Top University.
- Advanced to the finals in National Diving Championships.
- Successfully passed the CPA examination on initial attempt.
- Uncovered embezzlement scheme and helped devise a more accurate accounting system for summer employer.

List *four* examples where you have exceeded standards of excellence. Identify for yourself why *you* label them as accomplishments.

1. _____
2. _____
3. _____
4. _____

EXERCISE 10

Your Unique Profile . . .

PURPOSE:

To describe yourself.

DISCUSSION:

Part of your self-analysis is your development of a personal profile that expresses, in a fairly concise way, *who* you are. Employers ask for a personal profile for the same reasons that college and graduate schools ask for it, to see if you have a grasp of *who* you are and *where* you want to go.

You need to be able to say more than: "I am Willard Hunter and I'm a marketing major and a finance minor from Top University." You need to be able to provide some depth in your self-description. "I am Willard Hunter. My formal training is in the areas of marketing and finance, as well as economics, management and information systems. I have been an active person here at Best, having been a member of number of professional, social, and volunteer organizations. My personal interests involve athletics and outdoor activities, as well as reading, travel and theatre."

> By having made a statement like this, the student has shown first of all that he or she has thought about the way he or she might fit into an employment situation, and secondly, that he or she is willing to be an active, rather than a passive participant.*

Writing the *Personal Profile* is like answering the *Tell Me About Yourself* question in the job interview. Don't let it become a string of personal adjectives.

> Be able to discuss your personal characteristics by using information from your personal inventories. Don't try to emphasize characteristics that are not your strengths just because you think your employer wants you to be that way. Try to uncover your personal strengths and abilities.+

---

* Bolles, Richard Nelson. *What Color Is Your Parachute?* Berkeley, CA: Ten Speed Press, 1982.
+ *The Employment Kit: A Practical Guide to Achieving Success in the Job Market.* Chicago, IL: American Marketing Association, 1986. p. 3.

INSTRUCTIONS:

Write your own personal profile. Make it as specific as possible. Refer to Exercises 1-10. In addition, make your volunteering, extracurricular and leisure time activities statement more dynamic than that given in the sample on the previous page.

EXERCISE 11

Extracurricular Activities

PURPOSE:

To identify how experiences and responsibilities assumed in your extracurricular activities translate into the communication, organizational, and planning skills sought by employers.

DISCUSSION:

Many of the *jobs* you have had have been directly related to your involvement in campus clubs and organizations. You were not paid for accepting these responsibilities, and in many cases you enjoyed doing them. Ideally, you should find the same feelings of satisfaction in career jobs. This exercise is designed to help you in two areas:

- To recognize your accomplishments and to describe them in business language.

- To recognize your abilities, skills and talents and to decide how you can best make use of them in your career. As you examine these activities, try to identify career opportunities where you can use your strengths.

INSTRUCTIONS:

Make a list of all of your affiliations with clubs and non-Greek organizations. Include everything from high involvement with leadership positions held to minor involvement with small groups.

_____

_____

_____

_____

_____

_____

_____

Here are some examples of student activity descriptions. Each of these was placed in the **EXPERIENCE** section of the resume. Examine and discuss how each is effective or can be improved. Most of the sentences are short and begin with active verbs. They describe accomplishments and responsibilities, and include numbers when appropriate.

Samples:

Chairman, University Task Force on Greek Relations
Developed the University's first Document of Shared Assumptions between the Administration and the Greek organizations. The document covers topics ranging from management services offered by the University to establishing residence capacities of Fraternity houses.
Supervised the implementation of standards and policy.

Chairman, Budget Committee
Student Government Association
Participated in weekly meetings held to allocate funds from $120,000 budget to all university organizations.
Audited financial records of organizations applying for supplemental funds totalling $30,000.
Counseled organizations in improving money management.

University Tour Guide
Led a two-hour presentation of campus facilities twice daily.
Responded to questions and comments of groups of up to fifty people.
Improved public speaking and interpersonal skills while marketing the University to potential students.

Fundraising Chairperson
Residence Hall Association
Acted as business and community liaison.
Solely responsible for developing, organizing and directing a care-package fundraiser. Supervised 50 people. Received and handled 550 checks, resulting in a gross profit of $6000.

Print Journalist/Television Anchor
University Newspaper and Television
Received *Best Writer Award* for a feature article, *Look for the Poor.* As part of the television crew, anchored daily telecasts, produced commercials, operated cameras and edited film. Produced, edited and directed a multimedia slide show.

EXERCISE 12

Write Your Own Campus Activity Descriptions

INSTRUCTIONS:

Use the following work space to identify and describe your own extracurricular activity(s). Give your job title. On a new line, identify the organization. Construct a precise description, one that will give a clear understanding of specifics. Include statistics and strong action words, as well as accomplishments and skills statements. Use Appendices I, II and III.

Activity 1.

_____

_____

_____

_____

Activity 2.

_____

_____

_____

_____

Activity 3.

_____

_____

_____

_____

- NOTES -

EXERCISE 13

Greek Life

PURPOSE:

To translate fraternity/sorority experiences into meaningful job descriptions.

To identify the skills used as you performed these jobs.

To write descriptions which include both the *activity* and the *skill*.

DISCUSSION:

Some of you have been heavily involved with activities in your fraternities and sororities. At first you joined committees and participated in everything from sports to fundraisers. As you reached your junior or senior year, you may have been elected to leadership positions. Your peers and college administrators may have elected or appointed you to an Inter-Fraternity or Inter-Sorority Council. You may have represented *Greek Life* on a University Council. You enjoyed what you did. The following exercises will help you translate these college activities into attractive job descriptions. Recruiters will recognize your team, planning, organizational, and/or leadership skills. If you have strong *Greek Life* experiences, you may find it appropriate to place these descriptions in the **WORK EXPERIENCE** category on your resume.

INSTRUCTIONS:

The following samples have been taken from student resumes. Some have simply listed job responsibilities; others have greater depth. Rework each of the following so that activity descriptions become strong skills statements. Include numbers, percentages and all details that can make you an asset to a potential employer.

Let's take a look at these samples. In the space below each, list a skill(s) used in order to accomplish the task or goal. Construct a statement that describes the activity, and the skills involved in accomplishing it.

Sample:

Parliamentarian: Alpha Epsilon Phi Sorority
Supervised meetings according to Robert's Rules of Parliamentary Procedures.

Skill(s):
1. supervisory skills
2. listening skills
3. decision-making skills

Statement: Supervised meetings according to *Robert's Rules of Order*. Improved listening and decision-making skills. Made recommendations for proper use of Parliamentary Procedure.

EXERCISES:

Chairman of Standards Board: Alpha Tau Omega Fraternity
Directed the governing board of the fraternity. Supervised decisions regarding rules and regulations.

Skill(s):
1. _____
2. _____
3. _____

Statement: _____
_____
_____

Ombudsman: Pi Beta Phi Sorority
Acted as liaison between members of the sorority and the executive board.

Skill(s):
1. _____
2. _____
3. _____

Statement: _____
_____
_____

Chairperson of Program Committee: Kappa Kappa Gamma Sorority
Published weekly announcement sheets, monthly calendars, and chapter evaluations.

Skill(s): 1. _____

2. _____

3. _____

Statement: _____

_____

_____

Vice President: Sigma Chi Fraternity
Indoctrinated and trained 35 new initiates.
Chaired Finance and Executive Committees.
Coordinated alumni fundraising campaign.

Skill(s): 1. _____

2. _____

3. _____

Statement: _____

_____

_____

Pledge Trainer: Sigma Nu Fraternity
Designed program for education of new fraternity members in codes of civic responsibility and standards of fraternity life.

Skill(s): 1. _____

2. _____

3. _____

Statement: _____

_____

_____

House Manager: Delta Upsilon Fraternity
Allocated $11,000 budget. Selected contractors for partial renovation of house and grounds. Supervised expenditures of $5000 on the project. Managed 87 people efficiently.

Skill(s):   1. _____

2. _____

3. _____

Statement: _____

_____

_____

Vice President - Finance: Kappa Alpha Theta Sorority
Controlled sorority budget of $20,000 per semester for a membership of 100 women. Revised and implemented accounting system and reported to national office. Served on executive board of sorority.

Skill(s):   1. _____

2. _____

3. _____

Statement: _____

_____

_____

President: Beta Theta Pi Fraternity
Developed management skills through consultation with contractors and the Alumni House Corporation. Supervised maintenance and renovation of the Chapter House.

Skill(s):   1. _____

2. _____

3. _____

Statement: _____

_____

_____

EXERCISE 14

Write Your Own Greek Life Descriptions

INSTRUCTIONS:

List *your* leadership positions and *your* activities in your fraternity/sorority. Describe the work you do/did. Use accomplishment and skills statements. Begin each with a past tense active verb. Be as detailed as possible. Include numbers. Use the examples in this workbook *only* as a trigger for your own job descriptions. You want to be unique. You do *not* want to select from a menu of ideas.

_____

_____

_____

_____

_____

_____

_____

_____

_____

_____

_____

_____

_____

_____

_____

_____

_____

- NOTES -

EXERCISE 15

Make Your Leisure Time Activities Work for You . . .

PURPOSE:

To use specific language to pinpoint and explain your interests, hobbies, and talents.

DISCUSSION:

When you begin to self-evaluate in preparation for writing your resume, you may find that you have spent much of your free time pursuing special interests-- hiking, taking music lessons, participating in sports, traveling alone or with family, learning another language, collecting baseball cards, shells, rocks, etc. All of these experiences enrich you, and if you describe them precisely, they may generate strong interest in you as a job candidate.

Use this exercise to *upgrade the language you use* to describe these experiences and skills. Many recruiters begin an interview by referring to this section on your resume. They feel that you will relax when you describe what you enjoy. In order to generate a question, your special interest needs to appear on your resume in crisp, clear, detailed language. Your choice of what you do in your free time can reveal a great deal about your character. Be prepared to link your accomplishments in these areas with accomplishments you can perform on the job.

INSTRUCTIONS:

Here is a sampling of sports, hobbies and interests. It may "trigger" your thinking.

- reading
- tutoring
- travel
- computers
- handwork
- collecting
- Red Cross programs
- music
- photography
- exercise
- golf
- foreign languages

Choose at least three interests, hobbies or talents from *your own life experiences.* You are not limited to this list. Name the interest, hobby or talent. Move from a general to a precise description, one that will give the reader a clear understanding of *the specifics* of *who* you are and *what* you do. When you give details, you enable the reader to recognize that you have used planning, organizing, supervisory, and teaching skills.

Samples:

You may enjoy fishing. If you list "fishing" as a single word, you miss an opportunity to tell the reader that you have specific areas of interest. For instance, "fishing" or "skiing" can become any of the following:

- bass fishing
- fresh-water fishing
- deep-sea fishing
- alpine skiing
- water skiing
- cross-country skiing

A specific sentence may read: Make fly-fishing lures.

If you are interested in racquetball and tennis, why not describe your interests as racquet sports? Other specific descriptions of sports interests can become:

- Taught private tennis lessons to adults and children.
- Served as tournament official for National Girls' Tennis Championships.
- Organized and conducted tennis camps and clinics.

When you name your specific interests, hobbies or talents, give the reader a *picture* of who you are. Use specific numbers, details and descriptions.

Name it: _____

Specific description(s): _____

_____

Name it: _____

Specific description(s): _____

_____

Name it: _____

Specific description(s): _____

_____

Internships

PURPOSE AND SUMMARY:

Read Me! The listing of an *Internship* on your resume sends an immediate *green flag* signal to a recruiter. It says that you sought after and have been selected to take part in "a real world" experience. It may be in your academic field--accounting, public relations or law; it may be in government--state or federal; it may be in one of the local "helping" agencies. In many cases you become a "jack of all trades." You see how an organization works from the inside. You may or may not be paid for this work, but in most cases it is invaluable. There are benefits for all. The organization benefits because it gets a helping hand where it is most needed. *You* benefit for some or all of the following reasons:

- You find an opportunity to "test the waters" before committing yourself to a career field.

- You recognize that there are a variety of opportunities and "tasks" within your field. You will better understand where you will "fit" and be comfortable.

- You "network" with others who are working in the field. If permanent jobs open up, these "contacts" will know what and where they are.

- You get an inside look at the agencies of the federal, state and local governments. You may or may not plan to enter government service, but you will share an experience which will broaden your general knowledge. If you like what you see, you will support the system. If you dislike what you see, you can do something to better the system.

DISCUSSION:

The internships described in the following two exercises are *real*. Company names have been changed, but the descriptions have been taken from student resumes. They are included here to make you aware of the value and variety of internships available to you. Perhaps they will encourage you to apply for this form of *job experience*. Because they are *real*, you will find that the wording and the depth of the descriptions sometimes need reworking.

- NOTES -

EXERCISE 16

What Did You Accomplish During Your Internship?

INSTRUCTIONS:

Read each of the following samples and assignments. Many of the descriptions neglect to include accomplishment statements. As needed, expand the description to include accomplishments statements. Add new information if you feel it is needed.

Samples:

Intern
Global Textiles, Inc. Nazareth, PA
Computed raw material costs and forecasted 20% increase in monthly sales. Transferred computer-generated figures to ledgers for monthly financial reports. Handled business operations of a small, privately held company. Developed interpersonal skills with both management and vocational employees.

Intern
Tyler Business Machines, Los Angeles, CA
Designed and implemented a management control system for 42 contracts. Applied corporate communication skills while editing, publishing, and distributing a national news brief. Assisted in the organizing of a national convention. Managed a staff of 6 in the assembly and distribution of marketing tools for the national sales force.

ASSIGNMENTS:

Intern
Progressive City/Growing County Summer Intern Program
Worked at the Office for Economic Development.
Performed research to gather data on local businesses. Participated in visits to executives of these businesses to ascertain what assistance local government could provide.

Accomplishments statements(s): _____

_____

Student Intern
Savings and Loan Association, Sarasota, FL
Supported the development of a new tax accounting system in the accounting division. Aided data systems division in implementation of a new management information system. Contributed to preparation of quarterly and annual reports in the financial reporting division. Participated in the executive division's conversion of the association to a stock institution.

Accomplishments statement(s):_____

_____

Public Relations Intern
Presidential Center, Atlanta, GA
Coordinated media support materials for "Women and Constitution Conference." Prepared more than 150 press packages. Handled mailings for 500 tape requests. Designed efficient filing system. Wrote articles for and distributed in-house newsletter.

Accomplishments statement(s): _____

_____

Research Intern
Selective Securities, Inc., Greensboro, NC
Implemented first computer budgeting programs, database, and spreadsheet analysis. Assisted brokers in stock research and analysis. Gained working knowledge of securities field in preparation for Series 7 exam.

Accomplishments statement(s): _____

_____

Summer Intern
Candid Communications, Inc., Canton, OH
Assisted the coordinators, interviewers, and supervisors with all steps of the hiring process. Arranged applicants' test sessions, graded tests. Arranged appointments for interviews, physicals, and job offers. Assembled manuals for training programs.

Accomplishments statement(s): _____

_____

EXERCISE 17

What Skills Did You Develop or Enhance During Your Internship?

INSTRUCTIONS:

Some internship descriptions are nothing more than a shopping list of tasks completed. In the following exercise, describe how each internship benefited or should have benefited the receiver of the internship. What specific skills were used or enhanced as each task was completed? Refer to Appendix III.

Samples:

Editorial Intern
Fashion Newspaper, Atlanta, GA
International Trade Paper for the Wholesale and Retail Fashion Industry. Refined observation and interviewing skills while assessing retailers and manufacturers' latest fashion trends. Participated in editorial fashion shoots. Wrote business features.

Public Relations/Marketing Intern
NFL Football Club, Port Jefferson, NY
Wrote feature articles for *Winning* magazine. Developed public relations skills while preparing press releases and coordinated player interviews with national and local media. Produced media guide. Kept statistics and assisted with the organization of press facilities for NFL football games.

ASSIGNMENTS:

Congressional Intern
Subcommittee on Telecommunications, Consumer Protection and Finance. U.S. House of Representatives, Washington, DC
Intervened on stalled negotiations between U.S. and Soviet media agencies and successfully completed arrangements for a joint satellite-delivered television broadcast. Researched, analyzed and reported on the process used to ban cigarette advertising from television, and based on these findings proposed strategies to limit current beer and wine commercials.

List skills: _____

Write a skills statement:_____

_____

Intern
Foreign, Inc., Buenos Aires, Argentina
Developed fluency in Spanish while in foreign relations department of an international firm. Office duties required bilingual capabilities in oral and written interpretation. Interaction with clients provided background in international client relations and intercultural communication.

List skills: _____

Write a skills statement:_____

_____

Accounting Intern
Doud and Langer, Inc., Pine Hill, AL
Entered cash receipts for linerboard sales into the computer system. Maintained the miscellaneous cash receipts ledger. Invoiced linerboard sales. Prepared special accounting reports for upper management. Developed computer reports on daily paper billings and monthly waste paper transactions.

List skills: _____

Write a skills statement:_____

_____

Court Intern
Supreme Court of Nevada, Carson City, NV
Researched "judicial error" to create a proficient checklist for trial judges. Conducted extensive study on constitutionality of "Drug Courier Profiles." Observed criminal trials, oral arguments, and various other court proceedings. Court exposure increased research and organizational skills while improving my knowledge of the law.

List skills: _____

Write a skills statement:_____

_____

Merchandising Intern
Textiles, Inc., Fayetteville, NC
Merchandised junior and missy sportswear line. Provided support to product marketing by interacting with national retail buyers.

List skills: _____

Write a skills statement: _____

_____

EXERCISE 18

Write Your Own Internship Descriptions

INSTRUCTIONS:

Use the following work space to identify and describe your *own* internship(s). Name the internship. On a new line, identify the organization. Give a precise description, one that will give a clear understanding of *specifics*. Include statistics and strong action words. Include accomplishments and skills statements. Use Appendices I, II, and III.

1. _____

2. _____

3. _____

4. _____

Volunteering

DISCUSSION:

Increasingly, employers recognize that volunteerism enhances performance on the job and that people involved in challenging volunteer activities tend to develop strong skills in working with other people, problem solving, vision and leadership.*

A growing percentage of the *Fortune* 1000 corporations encourage their employees to get involved with volunteering in addition to holding down their full-time jobs. This alone should give you reason to include your volunteering experiences on your resume. Employers recognize that these kinds of experiences can turn followers into leaders, and increase self-confidence. Eleanor Reynolds and her husband, John Reynolds, the president of Outward Bound USA, co-wrote *Beyond Success: How Volunteer Service Can Help You Begin Making a Life Instead of Just a Living*. They encourage students to take full advantage of their volunteering efforts.

When you write your resumes, "don't be shy or apologetic about your service involvements. Be specific, describing not only your position but your direct contributions. Rather than saying you were responsible for organizing a yearly rummage sale, say that you organized a rummage sale that netted $5000 in revenue, an increase of 10% over the previous year."+

Skills and capabilities developed while you are working as a volunteer are often transferrable to the work place. It is time to assess them. You may be making decisions far beyond the authority you would enjoy in a paid job. You have more responsibility and more freedom to be creative. If you are not yet taking part in volunteering, research and seek out opportunities in your school or community.

Choose one which supports your career training. *Volunteer* for a group that needs you! Where can you do the most good? Where can you apply your skills, talents, and/or personal sensitivity? Enhanced job performance is a secondary result of volunteering. The first is a healthy dose of improved self-esteem.

---

* Thompson, Terri with Golden, Sharon F. "Volunteer Jobs with Solid Payoffs." *U.S. News and World Report*, April 24, 1989. p. 76.

+ Ibid., pp. 76-77.

EXERCISE 19

Volunteering Pays Off . . .

PURPOSE:

To recognize how your volunteering can lead to one or more of the following: new contacts, greater expertise, added skills, even a new job or career.

DISCUSSION:

Your volunteer work may be in full bloom as you organize fraternity/sorority or club activities on campus. In fact, you may be directing others. Skills developed in recruiting other volunteers and running training sessions often can be translated directly into corporate positions in human resources and community relations. Experience with volunteer income tax assistance programs may give you a direct line to a job with a "Big Eight" accounting firm. Highlighting such accomplishments specifically and descriptively on a resume is the best way to get service work noticed. Experts recommend listing skills and using statistics and strong, action-oriented words to describe your contributions. Recognize that volunteering provides frequent opportunities to assume leadership roles. In the **EXPERIENCE** section on your resume, list volunteer activities that are similar in structure to jobs.

Here is a sampling of volunteering activities. They may trigger your thinking.

- tutor
- hospital volunteer
- coach
- political volunteer
- soup kitchen

- Big Brother/Big Sister
- Humane Society
- Special Olympics
- Outward Bound
- civic association

INSTRUCTIONS:

Assume that you are affiliated with each of the following volunteering activities. Write a precise description for each. Be sure to include tasks performed, and quantify and qualify your accomplishments. What were the results of your accomplishments? Be resourceful and creative.

Samples:

President, PTA
Elementary School, Smithtown, NY
Supervised an association with 60 members. Increased membership by 20%. Formulated teacher support policies. Created a $5000 budget. Planned and implemented a successful fundraising campaign.

Secretary
WPPP Public Broadcasting System, Atlanta, GA
Wrote and sent a monthly newsletter to 68,000 members. Edited a conference transcript. Publicized the annual celebrity auction which netted more than $875,000.

EXERCISES:

1. Title: Vice President
   AIESEC: The International Association of Students in Economics and Business

   Tasks, accomplishments, and skills used: _____

   _____

   _____

2. Volunteer at John's Mental Hospital, Women's Hospital Auxiliary

   Title: _____

   Tasks, accomplishments, and skills used: _____

   _____

   _____

3. Volunteer with the Democratic Gubernatorial Campaign in Tennessee in 19xx

   Title: _____

   Tasks, accomplishments, and skills used: _____

   _____

   _____

4. Volunteer tutor, Children's Home

   Title: _____

   Tasks, accomplishments, and skills used: _____

   _____

   _____

EXERCISE 20

Write Your Own Volunteering Description

INSTRUCTIONS:

Choose at least three service jobs from *your own* life experiences. You are not limited to the list above. Name the volunteering experience. Give a precise description, one that will give a clear understanding of *specifics*. Describe each volunteering experience using statistics and strong, action-oriented words. If you are weak in this area, volunteer now!

1. _____
_____
_____
_____

2. _____
_____
_____
_____

3. _____
_____
_____
_____

To get help figuring out the skills, talents and interests you can develop through volunteerism, contact one of the 400 clearinghouses located around the country. Listed in the phone book as *Voluntary Action Center* or *Volunteer Information and Referral*, or in the Yellow Pages under *Social Services* or *Community Organizations*, these centers maintain volunteer job listings and will assist you in zeroing in on the field of opportunity most related to your goals, available time, and location.

- NOTES -

EXERCISE 21

Use Your Skills . . . in a *New* Game

PURPOSE:

To help you to identify functional and transferrable skills, and to examine how they can be applied in a new work environment.

DISCUSSION:

You *build skills* as you move through life. As infants you began by learning motor skills, like walking and talking. Later, you applied known skills to new experiences. If you *organized* your room at home, you transferred that *organizational skill* to your desk at school or to your locker. As you matured you used your communication skills as you met new friends at school or at work. Employers seek skilled applicants who can transfer their prior knowledge, abilities, judgment, proficiencies, training and practice to the workplace. They want people who can transfer skills, and use them in a new job.

INSTRUCTIONS:

Use Appendix III as you *add a skills statement* to each of the following job descriptions. In some cases you may want to rewrite the sentence to *incorporate the use of the skill* into an existing sentence. Or, you may need to create a new sentence to add a skills statement to the job description.

Samples:

Customer Service Representative
Serge Flannel Industries, Albuquerque, NM
Enhanced organizational skills while coordinating orders for men's suits. Planned cuttings for plant. Kept running inventory of fabric available, and daily inventory of unfinished and finished suits in IBM PC. Arranged shipping routes and dates for all orders. Updated 46 store buyers as to status of orders.

Shopping Investigator
Protective Services, Hometown, OH
Checked internal control at Baseball Stadium. Trained in memory and observational skills. Purchased many food items and checked to make sure they were rung up correctly.

EXERCISES:

Swimming Instructor
Community Services Association, Stone Mountain, GA
Managed daily operations of two swimming pools. Maintained security and safety standards for pools. As a Red Cross swimming instructor, taught beginning, intermediate, and advanced swimming. Maintained progress records for individual students and the Red Cross. Adapted specific strokes for handicapped adults.

Skills statements: _____

_____

Dispatcher
Fast Transport Corporation, Jersey City, NJ
Organized truck shipment routes. Kept records of available drivers and equipment. Delegated driving and delivery duties for more than 100 drivers. Received shipping orders from customers and interacted with customers when problems arose.

Skills statements: _____

_____

Sales Representative
Recycled Paper Products, Pelham, NY
Wrote orders for cards, stationery, and mugs. Fostered growth relationships with department managers in major stores including Bloomingdales, B. Altman, Gimbels, and Brentanos.

Skills statements: _____

_____

Partner/Founder
Student Discount Cards, Top University, Nashville, TN
Evaluated the need for the service, the audience, and the merchant advertisers. Succeeded in reaching 8000 students, 25 merchants, 1 sponsor. Gross income: $8000.00.

Skills statements: _____

_____

EXERCISE 22

Work Experience . . . A Discussion Exercise

PURPOSE:

To examine samples of job descriptions.

DISCUSSION:

Most of you have held full- or part-time, seasonal, and/or on-campus jobs. You learned to perform tasks and accomplish goals valued by future employers.

The following samples of job descriptions have come from *real* student resumes. Most list responsibilities and tasks performed. However, some *neglect* to describe the tasks in terms of accomplishments and skills used. Employers seek people who can transfer skills, and use them in a new job.

They also want you to be very specific about your accomplishments. Whenever appropriate, include numbers and answer the questions how, what, why, when and where as you describe each of your accomplishments.

INSTRUCTIONS:

Use these samples as a source for class discussion. Which samples need to be improved? Specifically, how would you improve each?

Samples:

Swim Team Coach
Swim Team, Hilton Head, SC
Communicated effectively with parents, district officials, and other coaches to develop and organize team. Supervised and instructed team of 80 swimmers. Scheduled and planned daily lessons for six swimmers' levels--from beginners to lifeguards. Conducted five weekly swim meets.

Computer Programmer
Top University Career Planning and Placement Center,
New Orleans, LA
Coordinated and created a new data system to update files on 10,000 alumni. Used Date Base III program on an IBM microcomputer. Suggested and developed new, more efficient alphanumeric techniques in file maintenance. Improved and updated the system regularly.

Public Relations Coordinator
Alumni Communications Center, Top University, Tyler, TX
Handled public relations and facility and service arrangements in the organization and implementation of 10 alumni reunions. Coordinated and programmed reunion events. Enhanced communication skills while working with alumni committees and local businesses. Scheduled 36 mailings designed to maintain alumni support and interest. Used macro system to maintain and review records and reports.

Sophomore Advisor
Top University, Albany, NY
Counseled freshmen students as an assistant to the Resident Advisor. Participated on the Sophomore Advisor Coordinating Board. As a member of the board, coordinated activities and reorganized the Sophomore Advisor selection process. Refined interviewing skills while screening prospective Sophomore Advisors.

Editorial Clerk
Federal Health Agency, Office of Public Affairs, Atlanta, GA
Printed and distributed daily publication, *The News*. Polished writing skills while editing speeches and public health information for use in *Dateline: CDC*. Pulled Associated Press news stories off wire service. Logged requests for CDC speakers. Interacted with media and press.

Restaurant Worker
The Wild Pizza Co., Redmond, WA
Kept accurate records of inventory worth more than $7000. Processed $2000 cash receipts at the end of each working week. Responsible for opening and closing. Worked well with customers.

Crew Chief
Akin-BackVan Lines Moving and Storage, Kansas City, KS
Supervised loading and unloading of direct shipments of household goods. Completed training course in the use of Caterpillar and Hyster forklifts. Received and stored incoming shipments. Earned certification in the operation of straight trucks up to 24,000 lbs.

Law Clerk/Runner
Ambush, Fine and Rambush PA, Richmond, VA
Researched court records. Maintained file library and delivered and filed documents. Sharpened diplomatic and communication skills.

Bookkeeper
Sagspring Hotel, Brewster, CO
Entered accounts receivable and recorded sales. Supervised housekeeping. Increased responsibility led to a 43% pay raise.

EXERCISE 23

Work Experience . . . A Writing Exercise

PURPOSE:

To use effective accomplishments and skills statements to qualify and quantify job descriptions.

INSTRUCTIONS:

Write accomplishments or skills statements for the following. What, if any, transferrable skills were used for each job experience? *Rewrite* job descriptions which begin with *responsible for, duties included, assisted, aided in,* or *gained valuable experience*. Add your own *new information* to make each job description specific and complete. Use the action word list in Appendix I. Select from the skills areas listed in Appendix III, or choose one that you consider more appropriate. Refer to the samples of job descriptions throughout this book.

Examples:

Carpenter
Grimy Construction Company, Raleigh, NC
Assisted in the completion of trim work on homes. Developed carpentry skills by executing tasks delegated by head carpenter.

Accomplishments statements: _____

_____

_____

Teller
Silver Dollar Bank, Alamo, CA
Responsible for processing monetary transactions in an efficient and accurate manner. Dealt with customers on a personal level and informed them of services offered.

Accomplishments statements: _____

_____

_____

Self-Employed
Lawn Service Specialists, Aberdeen, NJ
Founded and managed a residential and commercial lawn service. Duties included bookkeeping, estimating, advertising, and payroll. Contributed capital investment for purchasing of supplies and equipment. Trained and scheduled staff, controlled operating expenses, customer relations, and management. This lucrative business helped finance college expenses.

Accomplishments statements: _____

_____

_____

Amphitheater Host
Sandy Creek, Memphis, TN
Worked in marketing office answering phones and assisting with promotion. Transported performers from airport to hotel. Manned ticket gate. Ushered for concerts. Guarded backstage door.

Accomplishments statements: _____

_____

_____

Tennis Instructor
Forty-Love Indoor Tennis Club, Matawan, NJ
Private and group instructor. Concentrated on the individuals' weaknesses during private instruction. During group instruction, organized drills and tournaments to motivate students to improve tennis skills and participate in healthy competition.

Accomplishments statements: _____

_____

_____

Administrative Secretary
Future Business Machines Corp., New York NY
Arranged meetings and seminars involving FBM and customer executives. Processed internal and external business correspondence. Maintained timecards for approximately 35 executives.

Accomplishments statements: _____

_____

_____

Marketing Researcher
Research Corp., St. Louis, MO
Researched banking behavior and trends for financial institutions. Duties included organizing statistical data for evaluation. Dealt with people from all over the U.S., with greatly varying economic and educational backgrounds.

Accomplishments statements: _____

_____

_____

Assembly Line Worker
Alligator Supermarkets, Inc., Miami, FL
Viewed management of central produce warehouse for South Florida supermarket. Observed process from receipt of goods to final shipment. Gained valuable experience working in various facets of production.

Accomplishments statements: _____

_____

_____

Waitress
Golden Goose Restaurant, Lakenheath, England
Performed a variety of tasks associated with food preparation and food service. Developed communication skills with a diversified population. Expanded ability to deal with delegated authority.

Accomplishments statements: _____

_____

_____

Manufacturing Apprentice
Nut and Bolt Manufacturing Company, Laurel, MD
Used drills, lathes, and other heavy machinery. Calibrated products and parts. Developed an understanding of the importance of inventory and quality control in an industrial setting.

Accomplishments statements: _____

_____

_____

Umpire
Baseball Board of Recreation, Los Angeles, CA
Developed a sense of judgment and the ability to deal with emotional adults while caring for the young players.

Accomplishments statements: _____

_____

_____

Retail Sales Associate
Preppy Clothes, Yarmouth, MA
Sales Associate for professional men's and women's designer sportswear. Demonstrated ability to handle diverse customers. Created and organized effective merchandise displays, and participated in customer wardrobe coordination. Assisted in distribution of shipments and oriented new employees.

Accomplishments statements: _____

_____

_____

Horse Show Coordinator/Desk Receptionist
Champion Farms, Kensington, OH
Delegated tasks at weekend Horse Shows. Trained riders in intermediate and advanced riding in both English and Western styles. Disciplined two-year-old and yearling horses. Structured clients' files in computers. Organized yearly breeding assignments.

Accomplishments statements: _____

_____

_____

Researcher
Health and Science Editor, Channel 99 News, WTTT-TV, New York, NY
Developed ideas for on-air stories. Prepared stories for air, and assigned camera crews. Interviewed all candidates for filming. Researched background statistics.

Accomplishments statements: _____

_____

_____

EXERCISE 24

Write Your Own Job Descriptions

INSTRUCTIONS:

Use the following work space to identify and describe *your own* job experiences. Give your job title. On a new line, identify the company or organization. Give precise descriptions of your tasks, accomplishments and skills. As you plan the wording for the description, follow this thought pattern.

Task: What did you do?
Accomplishment: How did you complete the task?
Skills: What skills did you use, gain, or enhance from having successfully completing the task?

Begin each description on a new line, if possible. Start with strong action words. List most recent job *first.* Continue in reverse chronological order. Include dates, facts, numbers, statistics, quotas and honors. *Some of the statements that you have already written to complete previous exercises may be appropriate here.* If they fit into the job description category, use them here.

1. _____
   _____
   _____
   _____
   _____
   _____
   _____

2. _____
   _____
   _____
   _____
   _____
   _____
   _____

3. _____

4.

5.

6.

EXERCISE 25

Skills Self-Evaluation . . .

PURPOSE:

To identify the skills you have used most frequently in your life experiences.

To understand that if you have chosen to take part in activities that require these skills, you are probably pretty good at them.

To recognize that people are hired based on about 15% technical skills and 85% "people" skills.

INSTRUCTIONS:

List the skills which you have identified as appearing most often in all of your job descriptions, and in your school, social, and volunteering activities. Be sure to include both technical and "people" skills.

_____

_____

_____

_____

Write a two sentence skills description about yourself.

_____

_____

_____

_____

_____

_____

_____

Newspaper Advertisement: Help Wanted Section

The Ultimate Overseas Career

Forget the 9-5 routine. AIC's Career Trainee Program is our entry-level professional training program and your gateway to a challenging and satisfying overseas career. It demands an adventurous spirit . . . a forceful personality . . . superior intellectual ability . . . a toughness of mind . . . and a high degree of integrity.

Our intensive leadership training offers a wealth of knowledge for future Company managers. If you are action-oriented, have good interpersonal skills, the ability to write clearly and accurately, a strong interest in world affairs, and a Bachelor's degree or more with an excellent academic record, you could qualify.

You must be a US citizen willing to undergo an extensive background security check and medical and polygraph exams. Foreign travel, foreign language proficiency, previous residency or travel abroad, or military experience are plusses.

To apply, send us your resume, day and evening phone numbers, and a letter explaining your qualifications. We will respond in 30 days to those judged to be competitive for the Career Training Program and a possible future managing overseas operations.

Personnel Representative
P.O. Box 12345
Happy City, USA 56789

AIC is an equal opportunity employer.

EXERCISE 26

Write a *Mock* Resume . . .

PURPOSE:

To write a resume in response to a newspaper advertisement.

DISCUSSION:

The advertisement on page 82 appeared recently in a big city newspaper. The name and address of the company have been changed. This exercise will give you an opportunity to practice resume writing and to target your experience and accomplishments for a specific job. The highly focused resume is the most successful. Here are some of the concepts found in the ad. Write *your* job descriptions so that you highlight what is sought after in the ad.

- overseas career
- action-oriented
- integrity
- foreign travel
- writing skills
- adventurous spirit
- intellectual ability
- foreign language proficiency
- interest in world affairs
- interpersonal skills

INSTRUCTIONS:

Construct a resume in response to the ad on page 82. Follow the resume skeletons on pages 84 and 88. Create your own **JOB OBJECTIVE**. This is an advertisement which gives you the flexibility to choose a job title close to or in your own career field. The ad says simply that candidates who are accepted will go into a Career Training Program with a possible future managing overseas operations. The company makes no requirement for a specific undergraduate major. Perhaps they are seeking employees for all areas of the company. Here are some sample job objectives. You are *not* limited to them.

Samples:

Seeking a position in an international firm using language expertise, business and legal education.

International work with an agency involved in the placement of refugees and location of missing family members.

Seeking a management position in a multinational company which requires use of Spanish language skills.

Since this is *only an exercise,* you may complete the assignment *as if* you have foreign language proficiencies and travel experiences. Otherwise, use your own experiences and accomplishments. Be sure that this practice resume sends the message that you are an adventurous, action-oriented person.

Your Mock Resume Skeleton . . .

Name_____

Present Address: Permanent Address:

_____   _____
_____   _____
_____   _____

OBJECTIVE: _____
                    _____

ACTIVITIES: _____
                    _____
                    _____
                    _____
                    _____
                    _____

EXPERIENCE: _____
                    _____
                    _____
                    _____
                    _____
                    _____

                    _____
                    _____
                    _____
                    _____
                    _____
                    _____

                    _____
                    _____
                    _____
                    _____
                    _____
                    _____

OTHER DATA: _____
                    _____
                    _____

REFERENCES: _____

EXERCISE 27

Write Your Own Qualifications Statement

PURPOSE:

To help you to seek a career position that encourages the use of these skills.

INSTRUCTIONS:

Some employers ask you to write a qualifications statement, summary or letter. They ask you to explain why you are the candidate most suited for a particular job. Based on self-knowledge gained from having completed many of the exercises in this workbook, write a qualifications statement for a specific job. Choose your own job or apply your statement in answer to the specific advertisement. Be sure to include tasks, accomplishments and *skills*. State your job title in the space provided.

Sunday sections of big-city newspapers and national papers like the *Wall Street Journal* contain large detailed advertisements. Select from one of these if you choose to complete this assignment in response to a specialized advertisement. Remember to focus your qualifications statement on the employer's needs and to use some of the concepts found in the ad. Speak about yourself and highlight your personal and career strengths, talents, and character.

Recognize the difference between an **OBJECTIVE** and a **QUALIFICATIONS STATEMENT**.

An **OBJECTIVE** pinpoints the job you seek. A **QUALIFICATIONS STATEMENT** elaborates on why you are a good candidate for a job.

Here is an example of how one student wrote an **OBJECTIVE** and a short **QUALIFICATIONS STATEMENT**. She named her specific skills in her **OBJECTIVE**, and elaborated on them in her **QUALIFICATIONS STATEMENT**. Had she been asked to write a letter explaining her qualifications, as was requested in the ad on page 80, she would have to have included all three-- tasks, accomplishments and skills--in the letter.

Sample:

OBJECTIVE: A marketing position in a health care organization that allows for application of personal selling and negotiating skills acquired through previous work experience.

QUALIFICATIONS STATEMENT: Extensive experience in customer service and management including supervising, purchasing, merchandising, and promotional development. Consistent success in self-motivated work roles establishes reliability and persistence.

Specific job title: _____

If you are responding to a newspaper advertisement other than the one on page 82, attach the ad to this paper. Be sure to include tasks, accomplishments and skills. Highlight your personal and career strengths, talents, and character. Make this statement *real* for you. You may be asked for one. Have it ready just in case.

Qualifications statement: _____

_____

_____

_____

_____

_____

_____

_____

_____

_____

_____

_____

_____

_____

_____

_____

_____

EXERCISE 28

Write Your Own Resume

PURPOSE:

To write the first draft of your resume.

DISCUSSION:

Ideally, you should create a resume for each job you seek. To do this, you must design your job objective, skills, and accomplishment statements to support or answer a job description. If you are searching for a position that requires specific technical or academic training, like computer programming or accounting, you won't have to make many resume changes. You have to have had prior training *in the field* to meet the basic job requirements and needs of individual employers. However, if you are seeking a position in sales, management training programs, and any number of other fields, you will have to write your job objective and describe your experiences, using language that matches *their* descriptions of job openings.

Part of the job description for a Customer Service Representative reads, "If you have good mechanical aptitude and customer service experience, this opportunity is awaiting you." In this case, tailor your resume so that you highlight your experience in these areas. Another ad reads, "Writing skills a must. Requires experience in advertising, media, promotions, public relations, or a combination of these fields." Here is an opportunity for students to describe fully their experience planning, organizing, and promoting campus events. Some of you may have contacted hotels or bands where you enhanced your negotiating skills. Many students have the kinds of qualifications that employers are seeking, but they neglect to direct their resumes toward results. They neglect to translate their accomplishments into words which *jump out* and say, "I satisfy your employment needs."

INSTRUCTIONS:

Choose a newspaper advertisement *or* locate a job description in your Career Placement Center for a position that is in line with *your present* job search. It may be a summer or part-time job, an internship or a full-time position. Write your resume. Remember that you are smart to *use language found in the job description*. In many cases, employers are searching for attitudes, personality, and specific interests. For example, the employer in Exercise 26 sought job candidates with integrity who were interested in world affairs. You may find that your experiences outside the classroom and work environment can also reveal *WHO* you are, and *WHAT* you can provide for your future employer.

BASIC SKELETON: CHRONOLOGICAL RESUME

YOUR FULL NAME

Present Address
Box 1234
Best College
City, State Zip
(area code) 555-5678

Permanent Address
5678 Home Street
Home Town, State Zip
(area code) 555-1234

OBJECTIVE: A position as _____.

EDUCATION: Your College Name, College City
Degree: Name Major. Date
Grade Point Average: Place here or above, next to date.
Specify honors, including scholarships, honorary societies, Dean's List, etc.

Specify activities.
Include clubs, fraternal organizations, etc. Name leadership roles.

Consider placing *professional tasks* under EXPERIENCE, (e.g., Club Treasurer, Resident Advisor, Research Assistant, etc.).

EXPERIENCE: Place in *reverse* chronological order. Put your most recent job first.

Job Title
Name and Address of Employer   Dates.
Interweave task, accomplishments, and skills statements.

Proofread: Do *not* be satisfied with listing tasks, without including specific skills developed or polished as a result of having completed the task. Begin each job description with a past tense active verb.

Job Title
Name and Address of Employer   Dates.
Repeat for each additional job experience. Use format for writing job descriptions, as suggested above.
See Exercises 23 and 24.

OTHER DATA: Include specific information that will *benefit* an employer. Examples: Knowledge of specific foreign languages. Knowledge of computer hardware and software. Travel experience that will make you valuable to an international company. Volunteering, hobbies, and interests that reveal special character traits and talents.

REFERENCES: See sample resumes throughout the book and in Appendix VI for positioning and wording that suits your taste.

EXERCISE 29

Writing Your Resume Is a Developmental Process . . .

PURPOSE:

To obtain feedback from students (classmates and/or peers) who are also writing their resumes.

DISCUSSION:

One way to get immediate constructive peer feedback is to use the *Round Robin*. Circulate the first draft of your resume around the room. Let's assume that there are about 20 students in your class. Not only will you find that others will spot errors in your basic English, but they will also make suggestions to help you clarify job descriptions, or write strong skills statements. When you read 20 or more resumes, you get a feel for what works or looks best. On some, you like/dislike the wording; from others, you realize that you have neglected to include, on your own resume, some valuable information. All of you benefit from this *sharing*.

Before you circulate your own resume, look at the sample resumes that appear in Appendix VI. The second draft illustrates changes made after receiving advice and comments from peers. Descriptions grew in depth, and information appears in new locations to enhance clarity and provide greater impact on the reader.

INSTRUCTIONS:

Create a third draft of the student resume on pages 90 and 91. Enhance the content and the accomplishments and skills statements. If needed, change the way the resume looks on the page. Make an employer say, "You've got the job!!"

Circulate your own resumes. Give and receive comments. Work together to enrich each other's resumes. If you are not completing this assignment as part of a class, seek out a number of *others* who are also writing their resumes. You will find that first drafts need revisions. You may also realize that your resume needs additions, or you may find a better way of describing what you have accomplished. Go on to work on the second draft of your own resume.

First Draft

MATT P. JORDAN

PRESENT ADDRESS: Box 20000 Top University St. Louis, MO 63130 (314) 555-9137	PERMANENT ADDRESS: 100 Carlton Ct. Trenton, NJ 08888 (609) 555-5413

OBJECTIVE: To secure a position as an athletic coach.

EDUCATION: TOP UNIVERSITY,
Candidate for BS in Physical Therapy, May 19xx.

ACTIVITIES: Member of Varsity Basketball Team.
Won conference (UAA) championship.
Member of Pi Kappa Alpha Fraternity.

EXPERIENCE: LANDSCAPER, Joe Greene's Lawn Service, St. Louis, MO.
Started company with best friend and worked there for three summers. Hired employees after the second year of business.

LIFEGUARD, The Club Pool, Wahiawa, Hawaii.
Worked 50 hours a week and was the only lifeguard all summer. Was in charge of everything from pool maintenance to the collection of pool fees.

STOCK BROKER'S ASSISTANT, Johnson, Drux & Smith.
Learned about the buying and selling of stocks and commodities, also learned about the duties of a broker.

REFERENCES: Available upon request.

Second Draft

MATTHEW P. JORDAN

PRESENT ADDRESS:
Box 20000
Top University
St. Louis, MO 63130
(314) 555-9137

PERMANENT ADDRESS:
100 Carlton Court
Trenton, NJ 08888
(609) 555-5413

OBJECTIVE: A position as an athletic coach.

EDUCATION: TOP UNIVERSITY, St. Louis, MO.
Candidate for BS in Physical Therapy, May 19xx.

ACTIVITIES: Varsity Basketball Team.
Led team in scoring freshman year.
Won conference (UAA) championship.
Pi Kappa Alpha Fraternity.

EXPERIENCE: LIFEGUARD, summer 19xx.
The Cadet's Club at Schofield Barracks, Wahiawa, Hawaii.
Worked 50 hours a week. Maintained pool and surrounding area, collected pool fees, and was individually responsible for entire pool operation.

STOCK BROKER'S ASSISTANT, spring 19xx.
Johnson, Drux & Smith, Wahiawa, Hawaii.
Observed the buying and selling of stocks; sent stock transactions to traders over the computer, and contacted potential customers by phone.

LANDSCAPER, summer 19xx-19xx.
Joe Greene's Lawn Service, St. Louis, MO.
Started company and hired employees after the second year. Contacted customers, planned work schedules, paid salaries, and kept records for the company.

ADDITIONAL DATA: Lived in Germany for six years. Traveled extensively throughout Europe and Asia. Observed the culture and partricipated in a number of athletic events throughout Western Europe. Enjoy deep-sea fishing and reading.

REFERENCES: Available upon request.

Writing the Second Draft of Your Resume

PURPOSE AND SUMMARY:

You are ready to edit for specific focus, content, and language usage. As you rework the language and focus of your resume, ask the following questions.

- Does my job objective or qualifications statement encourage the recruiter to read further?

- Do I link my credentials, skills, abilities, and personal qualities to specific job objectives?

- Do my strong points catch immediate attention?

- Are my job descriptions and accomplishments statements in line with my resume's specific job objective?

- Does my resume suggest that I have positive work attitudes?

- Does my resume suggest that I get along well with others? Will I fit comfortably into an organization?

- Do I use the language of my target employer?

- Is my resume an autobiography or does it highlight my experiences and call attention to my accomplishments and their results?

- Does my writing style communicate clearly and use strong, action verbs?

- Is my resme easy to read? Did I proofread? Is it free of errors? Is there adequate and balanced white space?

- Would I hire this applicant based on this resume? Why?

EXERCISE 30

Choose Me!!

PURPOSE:

To evaluate the first draft of your resume. How can you better describe your academic, extracurricular, and work experiences so that the reader sees you as having unique credentials?

DISCUSSION:

In a *Wall Street Journal* article titled, "Where Excellence Is Par," James Sterba addressed the issue of why so many exceptional students received rejection letters from colleges. Well-rounded, straight "A" students with plenty of leadership experiences have been turned down by highly selective schools. Why?

> They (colleges) want a broth of brilliant and talented eccentrics. Better to be weird, genuine, passionate, radical, intellectual, and/or a totally awesome square. All around jock? No! Better to excel in one sport, be state champ, or set a record. . . . A's only count if they are in quality (tough) courses. . . . An applicant has to leap out and shout, "Choose me!" . . . Altruism is in. . . . Volunteering is in. . . . This is my life videotapes usually do more harm than good.[*]

Top companies also use specialized selection processes. They may not be looking for the extremes that Sterba describes, but they do seek out *unique* individuals. And, they introduce an additional requisite. Will this job candidate fit *this company's* "picture of a successful employee"? Recruiters don't always preconceive or label the special qualities that make one candidate superior to the others, but they recognize the winning combination of assets when they see them on a resume. It is up to you to construct your resume so that a future employer can read between the biographical lines to find your personality and character.

---

[*] Sterba, James P. "Where Excellence Is Par." *The Wall Street Journal*. March 31, 1989. pp. 26-28.

INSTRUCTIONS:

Place a copy of the first draft of your resume on your desk. Refer to Appendix I for a list of strong active verbs, to Appendix II for self-descriptive words, and to Appendix III for a list of skills. Move through each of your descriptions. Improve your style. Use parallel structure. Begin your descriptions with strong action words. For all but your present job, use the past tense. Edit for non-essential words and phrases. Are there too many adjectives? Can you *tighten-up* the sentence structure? Are you repeating? Refine and expand your descriptions on *your* resume. Include skills and accomplishments statements.

The student who wrote the following was Social Chairman of his fraternity.

Here are a few examples of how he developed his resume descriptions.

Samples:

First draft:	Budgeted social dues.
Second draft:	Budgeted and allotted more than $1800 per month in social dues.
You write the third draft:	_____

First draft:	Improved communication skills.
Second draft:	Improved communication and bargaining skills through extensive dealings with bands, agents, and school administrators.
You write the third draft:	_____

First draft:	Organized and planned annual charity benefit.
Second draft:	Organized and planned annual charity benefit. Scheduled conferences and meetings. Handled all correspondence, publicity and promotion. Designed souvenir booklet.
You write the third draft:	_____

EXERCISE 31

Qualify and Quantify Your Job Descriptions

PURPOSE:

To translate tasks performed into strong job descriptions.

DISCUSSION:

Although employers are interested in the tasks you performed in prior *working experiences*, they seek the specifics of your success while performing those tasks. They want to know *how many people you supervised*, or *by what percentage you exceeded your sales quotas*. They also want to know what skills you used or enhanced as you performed each task. What can you tell the reader of your resume that will indicate that you are a stronger leader than someone else who may have held a similar position? You are now ready to edit the first draft of your resume, to identify your special talents and abilities.

The resume on page 96 is effective and has eye appeal. However, it is predominantly task oriented. Discuss how you would change it to include stronger skills and accomplishments statements. Notice how many times the writer used the expression *Responsible for*.

INSTRUCTIONS:

If the first draft of your resume is overloaded with a list of tasks performed, use the following process to transform tasks into *winning* job descriptions. Improve your own wording for clarity and meaning. Advertise your accomplishments and sell your skills to a prospective employer.

Follow this process:

A: Transfer tasks into accomplishments statements.

B: Transfer accomplishments into skills statements.

C: Transfer *both* into strong job descriptions.

Sample: Task Oriented Resume

JAMES L. ABBOTT
101 Sherwood Forest
Euclid, Ohio 44117
(012) 555-5888

OBJECTIVE: A position in field of production/operations management or information systems.

EDUCATION: **Top University**, Cleveland, Ohio
January 19xx
Major: Management -- Major GPA: 3.0/4.0
Concentration in Operations and MIS
Minor: Economics
Assumed 80% of expenses through work, loans and grants

EXPERIENCE: **Digital VAX/VMS-Computer Lab Assistant**
USA Tech Inc., Cleveland, Ohio, Sept. 19xx to present
- File update and maintenance of VAX/VMS system
- Train students to use computer-based learning on personal computers

Teller I
NorTrust Co., Cleveland, Ohio, May 19xx to August 19xx
- Worked full-time summer, part-time school year
- Maintained and controlled daily drawer/vault cash flow of $15,000
- Provided customer service
- Handled commercial/personal deposits
- Wrote currency transaction reports for cash deposits/withdrawals over $10,000
- Responsible for weekly shipments of food coupons to main office
- Issued money order/official checks
- Responsible for operation of security cameras in branch
- Trained new employees
- Responsible for locking vault and closing the branch

Driver
Treeline Auto Parts, Mayfield, Ohio, April 19xx to May 19xx
- Responsible for inventory control and processing orders
- Supervised drivers and directed transportation strategies

Swing Manager/Crew Person
Bob's Burgers, Euclid, Ohio, March 19xx to April 19xx
- Supervised production and distribution crews
- Unloaded trucks and controlled inventory flow
- Maintained store and trained new employees.

PROFESSIONAL Society for the Advancement of Management
AFFILIATIONS: CWRU Commuters Association

WORKSHEET:

Experience #1

Task(s): _____

_____

Accomplishment(s): _____

_____

_____

Skill(s) used: _____

_____

_____

Job descriptions: _____

_____

_____

Experience #2

Task(s): _____

_____

Accomplishment(s): _____

_____

_____

Skill(s) used: _____

_____

_____

Job descriptions: _____

_____

_____

Experience #3

Task(s): _____
_____

Accomplishment(s): _____
_____
_____

Skill(s) used: _____
_____
_____

Job descriptions: _____
_____
_____

Experience #4

Task(s): _____
_____

Accomplishment(s): _____
_____
_____

Skill(s) used: _____
_____
_____

Job descriptions: _____
_____
_____

EXERCISE 32

Spice Up Your Language, but Keep It Simple!

PURPOSE:

To get rid of *empty* words and choose *power* language.

DISCUSSION:

The business of writing your resume and job search letters demands that you apply the following rules:

- Make every word count.
- Avoid pompous, unnecessary, or overused words and expressions.

Good business writing demands that you trim away the non-essential words to get to the heart of the message. If you can turn adjective and adverbial phrases into adjectives and adverbs, you tighten up your writing. If you eliminate non-essential adjectives and adverbs, you create an impact sentence. Avoid using expressions, "I feel," "I think," or "I believe" if you wish to produce a strong, precise sentences. When you use fresh language, free of trite and overused expressions, you create your personal style.

INSTRUCTIONS:

A. Rewrite the following wordy sentences. Break up into more than one sentence, as needed.

1. I have an intense and enthusiastic interest in the structure and in the happenings of the forest products industry in all parts of the country.

_____

_____

2. I think that my long-term domestic and foreign job experience, in addition to my college education specializing in Finance, not only qualifies me for a place in Citibank's financial training program, but can make me an asset to your company.

_____

_____

99

3. I believe that an enthusiastic and fresh mind could greatly benefit your prestigious company.

_____

_____

4. As a senior graduating from Top University in the foothills of the Rockies, this coming May, I am writing to explore the possibility of employment in your outstanding public relations firm.

_____

_____

5. If you grieve over the fact that even though today's college graduates are technically capable, they often disqualify themselves by their insufficiency in "people skills," then my education in Psychology and experience in dealing with diverse people and situations is evidence that I can become a valuable asset to your sales team.

_____

_____

B. Improve the underlined words or expressions in the following sentences. In some cases a one-word alternative may work.

6. With <u>advance planning</u> you will complete the project on time.

_____

7. The workmen at the automobile factory <u>assembled together</u> all of the parts for the new model.

_____

8. <u>Attached herewith</u> is my resume.

_____

9. Please let me hear from you <u>at your earliest convenience</u>.

_____

10. <u>Thanking you in advance,</u> I look forward to meeting with you to discuss my qualifications.

_____

EXERCISE 33

Skills Self-Evaluation . . . A Reevaluation

PURPOSE:

To reevaluate your Skills and Qualifications Statements.

DISCUSSION:

In Exercises 25 and 27, you were asked to list Skills and write a Qualifications Statement. In a sense, you were asked to write the *first draft* for both. Now that you have completed and reevaluated your resume, you have a better picture of WHO you are and WHERE you want to go. You also have a more precise understanding of your accomplishments and skills.

INSTRUCTIONS:

Reevaluate the first draft of your Skills and Qualifications Statements. Rewrite, and include credentials, accomplishments and skills. Add more specifics, more depth and edit for improved writing style. Be sure that it is focused for a specific audience, a specific job or perhaps a graduate school. Call it a Qualifications Summary.

Qualifications Summary: _____

_____

_____

_____

_____

_____

_____

_____

_____

_____

_____

- NOTES -

Job Search Letters

Your basic resume is finished!! Now it's time to get serious. You have a good idea of **WHO** you are and **WHAT** you want from life. You are ready to seek out the unique position which will enable you to achieve personal satisfaction and self-fulfillment. You know if, how much, and where you want to fit into society's *respect* and *prestige* value structure. You recognize that you must market yourself to a company where the job is right for you. A job you don't like in a great company won't bring you happiness. Be picky; ***buy yourself*** the right job. Choose and select.

In earlier exercises, you learned that many reviewers give resumes a 30-second scanning. If they like what they see, they move your resume on, for a more selective review. Now, *before* you present your resume, turn the tables. Do your own scanning. Ask questions! Know all about the job you'll be doing. Know if you respect and like the people: peers, supervisors, subordinates, and customers. Read all you can about the organization and try to locate current or past employers who will give you an honest evaluation. It is critical that *you choose* the job, the environment and the people you like. If you are satisfied, after your research, that this is the job for you, begin to plan your job search strategy. Your enthusiasm will flow through your focused resume and letters.

The term *cover letter* is quickly becoming obsolete. More and more employers ask job seekers to include a qualifications letter with their resume. See the advertisement on page 82. Some career management consulting companies teach candidates to write a *Letter of Introduction* or a *Market Letter*, and suggest that they be sent without a resume. In both cases they stress that these letters be specific and of personal interest to a prospective employer. One letter does not fit all employers.

Why not take a lesson from the workplace and turn the humble cover letter into a fine-tuned persuasive letter? Have it *sell* the candidate's qualifications and call it a *Marketing Letter*. In many cases, it is this focused letter that lands the first interview. Plan to send it with a resume, ***but write it as if it is to be sent alone***. There may be a time when the letter alone is appropriate; you will have it ready to go.

The Marketing Letter

Marketing letters work. They allow candidates to point out specifically why and how they can be assets to a company. They imply that you are willing to take the time to introduce yourself and to explain what you can offer. They give you an opportunity to expand your resume and to focus on the accomplishments and skills sought after by individual employers. Above all, marketing letters let you explain why you have targeted a company. You have done your homework to research the job; now you can let the employer know how much you know about the company.

General Rules for Writing a Marketing Letter

- Write your letter from an employer's point of view. Concentrate on what you can do for an employer, not on what that job can do for you.

- Send your letter to a decision maker. Use director's, manager's, and supervisor's names.

- Never send a letter:
    To Whom it May Concern:
    Dear Sir or Madam:
    Gentlemen: The boss may be a woman. Find the name you need by phoning the company or consulting a business directory.

- Select from among your accomplishments and skills; elaborate on those which match the particular job you are targeting.

- Avoid self-praise. Allow your quantified accomplishments and skills to speak for themselves.

- Be assertive. Don't say that you will wait for a reply, which may never come. State that you will contact them in the near future, in hopes of arranging a meeting.

- Use active and avoid passive voice. Sound energetic.

- Keep it short. Limit the length of your sentences and paragraphs. Do not exceed one page.

- Bullet strong points. Don't make the reader dig for information.

- Leave plenty of white space around your bullets and paragraphs.

- Use paper and envelope that match your resume.

- **EDIT and PROOFREAD.**

Guidelines for a Marketing Letter

Your Street Address
City, State Zip Code: No comma between State and Zip Code
Today's date

Individual's Name: Be sure to use Mr. or Ms.
Title
Employer
Street Address
City, State Zip Code: No comma between State and Zip Code

Dear _____: Be sure to use the colon.

The first line of the first paragraph should get attention with:
- An accomplishment statement
- A referenced statement (someone has recommended you)
- A researched statement (you have researched their background)

The first paragraph should also contain:
- The purpose of your letter: you are seeking a position as ___ with XYZ .
- A strong interest in your prospective employer without exaggerating. You are overdoing it if you say that you have *always* been interested in this company, unless you can back up your statement with facts.
- No mention that you plan to use this position for career growth. It may be true, but don't put it in writing.
- A transition statement that links your experience or training to the job.
- Evidence of how you can be an asset to his/her company.
- A lead-in to a series of accomplishments statements.

In the second paragraph:
- Name at least three accomplishments that fit with the specific position you seek. Be selective.
- Use short, crisp sentences. Name accomplishments that have a connection to the job you seek. Other accomplishments may be appropriate for other jobs.

Your third paragraph should reaffirm your interest and appropriateness for the job you seek.
- Request a meeting at his/her convenience.
- State that you will be in contact by telephone within two weeks. You may state that you will be in the area during a specific period of time, and you will make contact when you arrive in that city.
- Name specific dates. For example, write "during the week of March 15, 19XX," or "from December 15, 19XX, through January 15, 19XX," rather than "during the school vacation."
- Don't say you will call on a specific day of the week.
- When you give dates, be sure to include the year.

Sincerely,
Sign your name.
Type your name under your signature.

Sample - Marketing Letter: For Discussion

P.O. Box 22492
Top University
Atlanta, Georgia 30322
September 3, 19XX

Ms. Jennifer Hendricks
Internship Coordinator
Central News Network
750 State Street
Atlanta, Georgia 30031

Dear Ms. Hendricks:

As News Editor of *The Circle*, Top University's student newspaper, I have gained experience in writing, editing copy, and supervising others in a collaborative effort to meet a deadline. I believe that this exposure to a news environment would prove to be beneficial to you in an internship position with your company.

- My prior job and extracurricular experience reflect my diverse background in both communications and law.

- While working as News Editor for *The Circle*, I interviewed former President George Washington.

- Interned on Manhattan Cable's *Time Pieces* program.

- Interned with the Volunteer Aid Society for two years and helped perform research on polygraph testing at the Georgia State Capitol.

- Developed, implemented, and coordinated the Legal Agencies and Outreach program departments of University Volunteer.

- As a Resident Advisor, I was responsible for 28 undergraduate men and women.

I would very much like to discuss the possibilities of an internship with Central News Network. I will be contacting you during the week of September 11, 19XX, to schedule an appointment at your convenience.

Sincerely,

Thomas B. Jefferson

Sample Marketing Letter: For Discussion

12550 Chelsea Park Lane
Winnipeg, Manitoba R3T 2N2
CANADA
March 22, 19XX

Mr. Mark A. Monack
Director of Recruiting
Houseman Auditing, Inc.
125 Fullerton Avenue
Chicago, IL 60606
USA

Dear Mr. Monack:

My strong academic background, as reflected in my 3.97/4.00 cumulative GPA, and a major in Accounting qualify me for a summer internship with Houseman Auditing, Inc. I am from the Winnipeg, Manitoba area, but will be in Chicago for the summer upon the completion of my studies at Top University. I am confident that I have the knowledge and background necessary for such a position, and I am eager to apply them.

I will be graduating from the Top University with a BBA in Accounting in May, 19XX. My accounting classes, as well as other courses in the liberal arts and business, have provided me with an excellent foundation for an internship in accounting. In addition to my course work at the Top University, my summer employment experience with the Recreation Department has given me the reliability and flexibility necessary for such a position and will allow me to make an effective contribution to Houseman Auditing, Inc. Here is a listing of some of my accomplishments:

> Completed Financial Accounting, Managerial Accounting, and both semesters of Intermediate Accounting as part of the requirements for my major. Received a GPA of 4.00/4.00 in these classes.

> Acquired knowledge in other areas of business, including finance, marketing, management, and statistics.

> Worked for the Recreation Department for the past five summers, assuming increasing responsibilities each year.

I have enclosed my resume, which outlines my qualifications in further detail. I would welcome the opportunity to discuss my qualifications and the possibility of employment with Houseman Auditing, Inc. I will be contacting you by phone during the week of April 1, 19XX, to inquire about the availability of a position.

Sincerely,

Betsy Ross

Enclosure

Sample Marketing Letter: For Discussion

P.O. Box 35123
Top University
Kirksville, MO 63501
March 9, 19XX

Mr. Michael Moneypenny
Vice President of Finance
Future Tech
132 Boardwalk Road
New York, New York 10021

Dear Mr. Moneypenny:

Highly developed leadership skills, experience in retail sales, and extensive public relations work make me a qualified candidate for a summer internship with Future Tech. My present course work includes classes in finance, accounting, and management. I will be receiving a BBA in Finance from Top School of Business and Accountancy in May 19XX.

In addition, I have gained valuable experience in finance and accounting through my summer employment. My work as a fraternity officer has enhanced my leadership and planning skills. These qualities can make me a valuable asset to Future Tech. My accomplishments as a salesman and a fraternity officer include:

> Created a 14-week rush training program to enhance the interpersonal skills of fraternity members.

> Collaborated with treasurer to format and manage a fraternity budget in excess of $55,000.

> Analyzed customer's needs and designed appropriate audio systems.

> Drew up cost estimates and coordinated assignments for five employees.

I would like to discuss my qualifications for a summer internship with Future Tech. I am looking forward to meeting with you, and will contact you during the week of May 12, 19XX, to schedule an interview at your convenience.

Sincerely,

Andrew Scott Jefferson

Editing and Critiquing
Marketing Letters

PURPOSE AND SUMMARY:
After you evaluate the following letters, you should have a better idea of how to construct your own Marketing Letters. The Marketing Letter Guidelines, page 105, covered most of the basics, but here are a few more specifics.

- Spell names correctly. Is it Anderson or Andersen?
- Send letter to a decision maker. Place his/her title next to the name, or under it, depending upon space availability.
- Gain immediate interest. Your job is to choose the most appropriate first-line attention grabber.

    -- Accomplishment: Link your accomplishments and/or skills to those sought after by the employer.

    -- Referenced: Someone who has recommended that you write. Make sure that both persons know and respect each other.

    -- Researched: Make a statement which reveals that you have some special knowledge of the company and/or its employees.

- If you are answering an advertisement, pick up the language in it.
    -- Explain specifically why you are interested.
    -- Show specifically how you fit the employer's needs.
    -- Organize according to the requirements listed in the ad.

- If employers ask that you include a qualifications letter with your resume, they want to evaluate *your* writing skills and *your* ability to link your education and experience to the job target.

INSTRUCTIONS:
Edit and critique each of the following letters. Here are some of the areas which may consider. You are not limited to them.

- business writing form
- complete information
- correct usage
- grammar
- paragraph variety
- parallel structure
- passive voice
- punctuation for business writing
- *self*-centered message
- sentence variety:
    - structure
    - length
- spelling
- state abbreviations (see Appendix IV)
- the too many "I's" syndrome
- wordiness
- *you*-centered message

- tone or attitude:
    - persuasive
    - positive
    - aggressive
    - timid
    - begging
    - pompous
    - assertive
- vocabulary variety
- weak language usage:
    - feel
    - think
    - believe
    - could
    - would
    - should

EXERCISE 34   *What's Right or Wrong with This Letter?*

Box 1234
Best College
Anytown, Anystate 09876
June 1, 19XX

Ms. Merry Richman
Director of Personnel Management
Big Hotel Chain
5678 Main Street, N.E.
Big City, Anystate 54321

Dear Ms. Richman:

Experience as a retail sales clerk has prepared me to be adaptable to the needs of both personnel and customers. In addition, my work in the Benefits Department at Bigstore, Inc., and my education at the School of Business Administration at Best College, specializing in Personnel Management, qualify me for a position in your management training program. I can be a valuable asset to Big Hotel Chain.

My responsibilities as a retail sales clerk, and as an assistant in the Benefits Department at Bigstore, a major department store in the state of Anystate, included:

> Worked in eleven departments where I was required to devise perceptive sales techniques.
>
> Analyzed employee medical claims from nine retail stores in the state.
>
> Reconciled medical claims with insurance grants.
>
> Interacted daily, by telephone and in person, with customers and employees.

These responsibilities enhanced my understanding of personnel management. I would like to discuss my qualifications for a career in your management division.

I am looking forward to meeting with you, and will contact you during the week of June 6, 19XX to schedule an interview at your convenience.

Sincerely,

Bea A. Niceguy

EXERCISE 35　　*What's Right or Wrong with This Letter?*

P.O. Box 10000
Great School
Smalltown, USA
October 20, 19XX

Mr. Seymour Prophet, Partner
Tax Accounting Department
Prophet and Prophet Law Offices
5432 Banking Boulevard
Bigcity, USA 45678

Dear Mr. Prophet:

A structured business education in Accounting, and a willingness to learn qualify me as a candidate for a summer internship with Prophet and Prophet. I will receive my BBA in June 1989, from the School of Business Administration at Great School in Smalltown.

I have gained valuable accounting experience in my summer jobs including auditing, payroll, and inventory control. Through my experiences and education, I have gained analytical skills and a unique understanding of the business world. You may be seeking an intern with these qualities. Here is a listing of some of my past accomplishments which emphasize my initiative and determination to succeed:

> Processed and audited time card vouchers necessary for timely disbursement of 120 paychecks.

> Suggested, developed and followed through with reorganization of file system consisting of 30,000 charts. Provided easier access of records while saving time, money and effort.

> Successfully handled $1500 sorority budget.

> Participated in group fundraisers which raised more than $2000 for cystic fibrosis.

I plan to be in the Bigcity area during the last two weeks of December. I will contact you during that time to arrange for a meeting to discuss my qualifications.

Sincerely,

Rosebud Flowers

EXERCISE 36 *What's Right or Wrong with This Letter?*

Box 71130
64 Newcomb Place
Top University
New Orleans, LA 70118-5555

Ms. Clara M. Barton
Personnel Coordinator
Personal Financial Security Division
Long Life Insurance Company
P.O. Box 550189
New Orleans, LA 70236

Dear Ms. Barton:

My involvement with university organizations such as Sigma Chi Fraternity and the university Volunteer EMS, and achievement of a 3.92 cumulative GPA qualify me as an excellent candidate for your internship program. As a junior majoring in Finance at Top University, I have the educational background necessary for the positions in your Health and Claims departments.

After speaking with former Long Life interns Michael Mountain and Edward Hill, I know that my discipline and motivation developed through my activities in college will make me a valuable asset to your company. Some of my activities include:

> Served as Pledge Trainer for Sigma Chi Fraternity. Organized activities and fraternal education program for 35 members during an entire academic year.
>
> Tutored learning disabled children in areas of math and reading. Instructed children in physical education.
>
> Worked as a tour guide marketing the Top University campus to potential students and their parents.

I am very interested in your internship program and would like to discuss the opportunities that your company will be offering this summer. I will contact you during the week of February 17, 19XX to schedule an interview at your convenience.

Sincerely,

Otto Schweitzer

EXERCISE 37   *What's Right or Wrong with This Letter?*

```
                                    P.O. Box 22750
                                    Top University
                                    South Bend, Indiana 46634
                                    October 10, 19XX
```

Mr. Alan Brick
Senior Recruiter
Green Computer Machine Company
1197 Pecan Street, NE
Macon, Georgia 30000

Dear Mr. Brick:

As a project coordinator for the Top University Alumni Office, I oversee 36 informational mailings consisting of more than 6000 documents. In addition, I act as a liaison between Top University and 800 Dental and MBA alumni, and have created a record-keeping system on our computers.

Your sales and marketing program may be in need of someone with my organizational skills. Some of my other accomplishments are:

- Maintained and updated more than 12,000 special customer accounts with one of the Midwest's largest department store chains.

- Provided sales and service assistance to customers.

- Raised more than $20,000 for the Campaign for Top, as a telephone solicitor.

- Maintain financial records for Residence Hall as Vice-President and Treasurer.

Perhaps we could meet to further discuss the value of my qualifications for Green Computer Machine Company. I will be in the Atlanta area during the week of October 20, 19XX and will call you to set up a meeting at your convenience.

                                    Sincerely,

                                    Kevin Rickwood

EXERCISE 38 *What's Right or Wrong with This Letter?*

P.O. Box 23171
Best College
Houston, Texas 77004
November 30, 19XX

Ms. Martha Dugan
Manager of College Recruiting
Human Resources Division
Super Union Corporation
Charlotte, North Carolina 28288

Dear Ms. Dugan:

Through my research of Super Union Corporation I have found that you have an outstanding Associates Training Program. My work experience and educational background in Finance makes me a valuable asset to you. I can bring to Super Union a harmonious combination of interpersonal and analytical skills.

These are my accomplishments:

- Assisted in the preparation of monthly financial statements for ten different companies while working as an Administrative Assistant at Wonderful and Company.

- Trained three secretaries.

- Tutored students in my financial and managerial accounting courses.

- Communicated with 200 members of Houston's business community while seeking prizes to be awarded at the Disabled Children's House fundraiser.

I would like to discuss the possibilities of entering the Associates Program at Super Union Corporation. I will call you during the week of December 11, 19XX to arrange a meeting to discuss my qualifications.

Sincerely,

Meghan Goodfellow

EXERCISE 39 *What's Right or Wrong with This Letter? First Draft*

112 Steeplechase Lane
Lexington, KY 40502
January 21, 19XX

Mr. Action Jackson
Senior Vice President and Chief Marketing Officer
Well Known Athletic Shoe Company
2295 Kings Street
Canton, VT 05021

Dear Mr. Jackson,

I was referred to you by my father, John Bigwig, President of State Gas and Electric, who has done business with Barry Smart. I am interested in an entry-level marketing position with Well Known Athletic Shoe Company.

Experience in related positions has equipped me with the fundamental skills needed for a position in your firm. My interest in marketing in addition to my education, work experience, and ability to interact effectively with others qualify me as a candidate for your marketing team.

My enthusiasm in the field of marketing lead me to the enrollment in one of the nation's leading business schools at the Best College. While following my concentration in marketing, I have

- Earned a cumulative grade point average of 3.61/4.0
- Awarded Dean's List
- Self-taught knowledge of Lotus 1-2-3

My work experience with Buyit Advertising Agency in Lexington and Brain, Wash, and Cashin Associates in Boston I demonstrated my motivation for added responsibility. I organized promotions, coordinated preliminary market research, and took part in a thorough analysis of primary and secondary data. I completed these tasks in a timely and efficient manner, and was frequently acknowledged by my superiors. This feedback is indicative of my ability to put forth the extra effort needed to complete projects with positive results.

I possess effective communication skills and the ability to work well with others. These qualities are demonstrated through my participation in the various volunteer programs.

My business education, work experience and outgoing personality qualify me as a strong candidate for your organization. I would like to arrange an interview with you in the near future in order to discuss a potential position with your company.

Sincerely,

Tiny Bigwig

EXERCISE 40 *What's Improved in This Letter? Do You See a Need for Further Changes? Second Draft*

112 Steeplechase Lane
Lexington, KY 40502
January 21, 19XX

Mr. Action Jackson
Senior Vice President and Chief Marketing Officer
Well Known Athletic Shoe Company
2295 Kings Street
Canton, VT 05021

Dear Mr. Jackson:

Barry Smart, your Retail Director, suggested that I write to you. He has done business with my father, John Bigwig, President of State Gas and Electric. I am currently seeking an entry level marketing position with Well Known Athletic Shoe Company.

I am completing my senior year as a marketing major at the Best College in Lexington. My academic and work experience reflects my success in college and strong interest in marketing. The following are some of my accomplishments:

- Earned a cumulative grade point average of 3.61/4.0
- Participated in group projects at both Buyit Advertising Agency in Lexington and Brain, Wash, and Cashin Associates in Boston
- Awarded Dean's List
- Self-taught knowledge of Lotus 1-2-3
- Organized extensive promotions for McBurger Food Franchise
- Coordinated, gathers and analyzed primary and secondary market research for a major account

I completed these tasks in a timely and efficient manner and was frequently acknowledged by my superiors. In addition, my volunteer work while at Best College demonstrates effective communication skills and the ability to work well with others.

My business education and solid work experience qualify me as a strong candidate for your organization. I can be in Vermont at a time convenient to you and will call within the next week to arrange an interview.

Sincerely,

Tiny Bigwig

EXERCISE 41   *What's Right or Wrong with This Letter?*

5000 Long and Winding Road
Mytown, USA   12345
June 1, 19XX

Mr. Bill U. Later, Vice President
Director of International Accounts
BigBank of Big Town
101 Big Road
Big Town, USA 78910

Dear Mr. Later:

My fluency in Spanish and diverse job experience make me a qualified candidate for an internship with BigBank of Big Town. As a Junior, I have studied Financial Accounting for two years. Also, I have an extensive liberal arts education. My 3.5 GPA is proof of my dedication and ambition in the pursuit of these studies.

You may be interested in a student eager to affiliate with a successful financial institution as a summer intern. My prior job experience reflects my diverse background in both bookkeeping practices and public relations. Here are some of my accomplishments:

> Brought journals and ledger with backlogs of 2.5 months up to date in just three weeks. This included all check and cash disbursements.

> Operated a successful small business. Handled all cash receipts and managed/counseled three employees.

> Interned with a Smalltown law firm. Coordinated the daily schedules of four runners.

> Worked in the foreign relations department of Foreign, Inc. in Buenos Aires, Argentina for three months.

I would very much like to discuss the possibilities for an internship with BigBank of Big Town for this summer. I will be contacting you during the week of June 6, 19XX to arrange an interview at your convenience.

Sincerely,

Spring Summers

EXERCISE 42

Write Your Own Marketing Letter . . .

PURPOSE:

To write a marketing letter to be sent with a resume.

DISCUSSION:

Read the job advertisement on page 82. It asks for a qualifications letter in addition to your resume. As you know, there are a number of labels given to this kind of letter. It is also known as a cover letter, a letter of introduction, or a qualifications letter. No matter what it is called, it is your opportunity to link *your* training and experience to *their* specific requirements and needs. Expand your experience descriptions to explain how and why you are most qualified for the job.

INSTRUCTIONS:

Write a letter explaining your qualifications to answer the ad on page 82, or write a marketing letter to be sent an employer of your choice. Plan to send it with your resume.

Before you begin, refer to the marketing letter guidelines, pages 104-109. Reread the resume exercises and use the resumes you constructed. All should be of help to you as you construct your letter. Look through the sample marketing letters, pages 106-108, and those in Exercises 34-41, pages 110-117. Some of them may give you ideas for persuasive tone and format. Use the space below for your first draft.

Thank You or Follow-Up Letters

Most senior executives say that *thank you* letters are an essential part of the job hunt. Many will not hire a candidate who has not sent a follow-up letter. In addition, and most importantly for you, this is your last chance to sell yourself, to shine, to expand on why you are the most suitable candidate for the job.

Sending a follow-up letter after an interview is basic business etiquette. It makes you stand out. You are remembered, and your letter is placed on the top of your file. You prove that you are genuinely interested in the position.

Be careful, however. Don't push too hard. There are two extremes. Some students, especially those seeking internships or summer positions, tell potential employers that the *job* will give them (the students) good experience. This may be true, but why put it in writing? After all, employers are looking for *workers*, not *users*. Begin any new *work experience* with the intention of applying fully your training, skills, and talents. *Experience* is a secondary benefit of a job well done. Other students will use the thank you letter to beg for the job.

Study your potential employer. Your letter should be a genuine message of thanks from one individual to another. If it comes across as insincere, you miss the purpose of writing it. Thank the interviewer honestly and graciously. Very few people reject a sincere expression of gratitude.

Guidelines for a Thank You Letter

Your Street Address
City, State Zip Code: Do not place a comma after State.
Today's Date

Individual's Name
Title
Employer
Street Address
City, State Zip Code: Do not place a comma after State.

Dear_____: Use a colon for business letter.

Your opening paragraph should:

- Thank the interviewer for meeting with you, without apologizing for taking the time.
- Mention the interview date and the specific job for which you interviewed.
- Refer to something which made the meeting especially valuable for you (e.g., meeting other people, a specific description of some aspect of the job which impressed you, any new knowledge about the industry or the company's future plans, etc.).

In the second paragraph:

- Reaffirm your interest in the position, and restate one or more of the reasons why you are a top candidate for the position. Here is your last opportunity to emphasize one or two of your qualifications--*to sell yourself*. This will remind the interviewer of why you can be an asset to his/her company.
- You may ask a question about something that was not covered during the interview.
- You may state that you are returning some documents that the interviewer asked you to complete.

Close the letter by restating your interest in the company. This lets the interviewer know you are genuinely interested in a position with his/her firm. Be sure to name the company.

Sincerely,

Sign your name.
Type your name under your signature.

Sample Thank You Letter: For Discussion

12550 Chelsea Park Lane
Winnipeg, Manitoba R3T 2N2
CANADA
March 30, 19XX

Mr. Mark A. Monack
Director of Recruiting
Houseman Auditing Inc.
125 Fullerton Avenue
Chicago, IL 60000
USA

Dear Mr. Monack:

Thank you for meeting with me on March 29, 19XX, concerning a summer internship position with Houseman Auditing Inc. The discussion we had was both enjoyable and informative. I also found the informal conversations with your junior accountants to be very beneficial.

By working for the Recreation Department for the past five summers and assuming increasing responsibilities each year, I have proven that I am flexible, reliable, and ambitious. These qualifications will make me a valuable asset to Houseman Auditing Inc. Furthermore, I am confident that my strong academic background from Top University, as reflected in my 3.97/4.00 cumulative GPA, has given me the knowledge necessary for a position with Houseman Auditing Inc. I am eager to apply it.

Our conversation has confirmed my interest in an internship position with Houseman Auditing Inc. If I can provide you with any further information, please feel free to contact me. I look forward to hearing from you soon.

Sincerely,

Betsy Ross

Sample Thank You Letter: For Discussion

P.O. Box 35123
Best College
Kirksville, MO 63501
March 9, 19XX

Mr. Michael Moneypenny
Vice President of Finance
Future Tech
123 Boardwalk Road
New York, New York 10000

Dear Mr. Moneypenny:

Thank you for considering me for an internship in your Environmental Concerns department. I enjoyed our meeting on Wednesday, February 20, 19XX. Our discussion was very helpful in answering questions I had regarding opportunities at Future Tech and your department.

I was very impressed with your training program for new employees. Having trainees work with experienced analysts on current environmental projects sounds like a very exciting way to gain valuable experience in management. Through my studies in Forest Management at Best, I am accumulating a broad understanding of the world's needs and the analytical and people skills necessary to pursue a career in environmental protection.

My meeting with you and your associates has convinced me that a summer internship with Future Tech would give me an opportunity to apply experience in timber management while in a professional setting. I look forward to hearing from you soon.

Sincerely,

Andrew Scott Johnson

Sample Thank You Letter: For Discussion

P.O. Box 21758
Best College
York, PA 17405
March 1, 19XX

Mr. Charles Stream
Vice President of Finance
Wood Associates
5625 Oakbrook Drive
Memphis, TN 30000

Dear Mr. Stream:

Thank you for considering me as a candidate for your internship program. I enjoyed meeting with you on Monday, February 27, 19XX and appreciated the tour of your office complex. The new wing in your office is very impressive.

I believe that my experience as the marketing director of an international business organization and my position as an assistant sales manager can make me a valuable asset to your brokerage firm. Furthermore, the communication and selling skills which I am gaining at Best College through classwork and various organizations make me a worthy candidate for your internship program.

Our conversation and discussion on the management consulting opportunities available at Wood Associates has increased my desire to work for your firm. If I can provide you with any further information, please contact me. I look forward to hearing from you soon.

Sincerely,

Nicole A. Fields

Editing and Critiquing
Thank You and Follow-Up Letters

PURPOSE AND SUMMARY:

Even if your interview has gone well, and you rate it as a friendly experience, your thank you or follow-up letter must follow proper business letter form. It is *not* a friendly letter. The company receiving it will include it in your files. If you are a prime candidate for a job opening, your letter will most probably be circulated among decision-making company personnel. You want your letter to be grammatically perfect. In addition, it must also reflect your positive *tone* or *attitude*. It should neither *beg* nor be overly *pompous*. Be assertive, but not aggressive. Present specific reasons for claiming job qualifications.

The following exercises ask you to make changes in sample letters to enhance readability. In some cases, you will need to correct usage, spelling, punctuation, and/or business letter form. Some sentences may be too *wordy* or too long. Some may be incomplete sentences. For example, the letter to Mr. Carroll has some well-written sentences, but the writer leaves out necessary information. You don't know if Mr. Carroll works alone or for a company. What is Mr. Carroll's job title? Nowhere does this writer name the specific position he is seeking. All you know is that he wants to be Mr. Carroll's assistant. You *assume* that it may have something to do with accounting. The writer refers to *skills* acquired in the VITA program, but doesn't identify specific skills. This is his last opportunity to name the skills, talents, and experience that qualify him for a specific job.

INSTRUCTIONS:

Edit and critique each of the following letters. Here are some of the areas which you may consider. You are not limited to them.

- business writing form
- complete information
- correct usage
- grammar
- paragraph variety
- parallel structure
- passive voice
- punctuation for business writing
- *self*-centered message
- sentence variety:
    - structure
    - length
- spelling
- state abbreviations (see Appendix IV)
- the too many "I's" syndrome
- wordiness
- *you* -entered message

- tone or attitude:
    - persuasive
    - positive
    - aggressive
    - timid
    - begging
    - pompous
    - assertive
- vocabulary variety
- weak language usage:
    - feel
    - think
    - believe
    - could
    - would
    - should

EXERCISE 43   *What's Right or Wrong with This Letter?*

770 E. Confederate Ave
Cambridge, Mass. 02139
March 21, 19XX

Mr. Eugene Carroll
10 North 14th St
Santa Barbara, CA 93060

Dear Mr. Carroll,

Thank you for meeting with me on March 16, 19XX. I enjoyed our luncheon at The Plaza and the informal conversation that followed. The location of your new office in the historic downtown area is wonderful.

I was impressed with the new accounting software program you have chosen to make your move easier. I am familiar with the older version of the same program, having used it with my former employer. Furthermore, the skills I acquired in the VITA program and my education at Top University make me a well qualified candidate to be your assistant.

If I can provide you with any further information, please contact me. Our meeting with you has confirmed my interest in working for you. I look forward to hearing from you soon.

Sincerely,

Hugh Hire Meeh

EXERCISE 44   *What's Right or Wrong with This Letter?*

P.O. Box 22856
Best College
Hanover, NH   03755
October 26, 19XX

Mr. Michael Stephens
Director of Accounting
Huxtable and Cosby Law Offices
815 Falconhood Lane
Augusta, GA   30901

Dear Mr. Stephens:

Thank you for considering me for the position of summer intern in your Criminal Law Department. I enjoyed meeting you last Friday October 23, 19XX, and appreciate you taking the time from your tax study to see me.

I feel confident that my Political Science background acquired at Best College, as well as my exposure to the Volunteer Legal Aid Club qualifies me for the research intern position at Huxtable and Cosby Law Offices.

After meeting you and observing your law clerks work together, my interest in being a contributing member of the criminal law department with your firm has been confirmed. I look forward to hearing from you soon.

Sincerely,

Rose E. Glaser

EXERCISE 45   *What's Right or Wrong with This Letter?*

1 Auburn Court
Union, N.J. 07083
May 19, 19XX

Mr. Hugh B. de Boss
Tax Accounting Department
Jetson, Flintstone, Rubble, and Slate Law Offices
400 North Main Street
Spring Valley, N.Y. 10977

Dear Mr. de Boss:

Thank you for meeting with me on May 13. 19XX to discuss my interning for you this summer. Our conversation and tour of your office increased my desire to work for Jetson, Flintstone, Rubble, and Slate Law Offices as an intern this summer.

The atmosphere of your office was very suitable to the working environment I am looking for. I felt comfortable speaking with you because our interests are so common. As an intern at this law office, I would feel very relaxed because the attorneys have expressed an interest to help me achieve a valuable learning experience.

The skills which I have acquired while majoring in Accounting at Best College and my internship at the County Public Defender's Office qualify me for an internship at the Jetson, Flintstone, Rubble, and Slate Law Offices. I look forward to hearing from you soon.

Sincerely,

Ima Jobbhunter

EXERCISE 46 *What's Right or Wrong with This Letter?*

1298 Windridge Drive
Erie, Penna. 16541
March 21, 19XX

Ms. Iwana Givuajob
Branch Vice President
Very, Very Big Corporation
8810 Bigco Drive
Durham, NC 27707

Dear Ms. Givuajob:

Thank you for taking the time to discuss the possibility of my summer internship with your firm. I learned quite a bit from our meeting, and was quite impressed with the efficient nature of your branch. I especially appreciated the opportunity to talk with some of your managers in order to get a feel for how things work at your Very, Very Big Corporation office.

After visiting your branch. I am confident that my enthusiasm and fresh outlook upon matters would be an asset to you and to the Very, Very Big Corporation you work for. I am a hard worker, as my 3.2 GPA might reflect. Yet, I have always worked hardest in those areas which genuinely interest me, and I am fascinated by the work you do at Very, Very Big Corporation. The diligence and enthusiasm that I will show should prove valuable to your Very, Very, Big office.

Please do not hesitate to contact me if I can provide you with any other information. I look forward to hearing from you soon.

Sincerely,

Dawn Juana B. Small

EXERCISE 47   **What's Right or Wrong with This Letter?**

1 Central Ave
Detroit, Mich. 48226
December 25, 19XX

Mr. Count deMonee
Greedee, Schiester, and Crook Investments
559 Laughingallthe Way
Tothebank, ND 58106

Dear Mr. deMonee:

I would like to thank you for interviewing with me on Friday, May 13, 19XX. Our conversation concerning an entry-level position with your firm in the money management department has inspired me to even more to pursue a career in this area. In addition, the opportunity to work with your contacts in Switzerland is very interesting to me.

I am confident that my background in business and my previous experience will enable me to be an asset to your company this summer. While interning at Financial Swindlers Corporation, I was able to receive an understanding of the workings of a financial institution. Furthermore, my speaking skills in French will be of great importance to your international department.

My meeting with you has confirmed my interest in Greedee, Schiester, and Crook Investments. I look forward to hearing from you soon.

Sincerely,

Ima Hood

EXERCISE 48 ***What's Right or Wrong with This Letter?***

Box 71130
64 Newcomb Place
Top University
New Orleans, LA 70118-5555

Ms. Claire M. Barton
Personnel Coordinator
Personal Financial Security Division
Long Life Insurance Company
P.O. Box 550189
New Orleans, LA 70236

Dear Ms. Barton:

Thank you for meeting with me on February 24 concerning your summer internship positions in your Health and Claims departments. I enjoyed talking with you, Ms. Turner, and Mr. Grant about what your company has to offer college students like myself.

Allowing your interns to actively participate in your operations, rather than simply observe, is impressive and encouraging. I am confident that my sense of responsibility and self-motivation gained through my involvement with Sigma Chi, Top University Volunteer EMS, and the summer camp at The Gap School will make me an asset to your internship program. Moreover, the skills I have acquired at Top University and my academic achievements, as reflected in my 3.92 GPA, make me a well qualified candidate for one of your internship positions.

If I can provide you with any further information, please contact me. I look forward to hearing from you soon.

Sincerely,

Otto Schweitzer

EXERCISE 49 *What's Right or Wrong with This Letter?*

4296 Oxford Drive
Decatur, GA 30309
June 1, 19XX

Mr. Harrison Eton
Vice President of Marketing
Alex Overseas Corporation
1409 Sunset Boulevard
New York, NY 11787

Dear Mr. Eton:

Thank you for meeting with me on April 6, 19XX. Our conversation, and a discussion with Mr. Richard Cambridge, increased my desire to work for Alex Overseas Corporation as a Product Manager in your Advertising and Marketing Division.

I am confident that my background in European and American Markets will make me a valuable asset to Alex Overseas. While working in the Sales Department at Alex Overseas for two summers, I gained in-depth understanding in inter-company sales and transfers. Furthermore, the skills which I acquired at Top American University and my academic expertise, as reflected in a 3.8 GPA, make me a well qualified candidate for the opening at Alex Overseas Corporation.

As an intern at Alex Overseas, I felt comfortable with being part of the team. I am glad you invited me back for a second interview and look forward to seeing you soon.

Sincerely,

Charles Windsor

EXERCISE 50   *What's Right or Wrong with This Letter?*

403 Gangster Way
Atlanta, GA 30344
June 1, 19XX

Mr Jason Baxter, Vice President
Director of International Finance
A Big Financial Corporation
Post Office Box 1224
Union, NJ 07083

Dear Mr. Baxter:

Thank you for considering me for a management position in your International Finance Department. I enjoyed our meeting on Thursday, May 20, 19XX. Your plans for your new Italian operation are impressive. I enjoyed the tour of your offices and the informal conversation with your staff.

I was most impressed with the effective manner in which you have adapted the management-by-objective system to your daily operation. This philosophy suits my interests and training. My concentrated study of Finance and Management acquired at The School of Business Administration at Top University has given me strong academic preparation. My work experience in the International Offices at C.M.I Enterprises, qualifies me for the position currently available at A Big Financial Corporation.

If I can provide you with any further information, please contact me. My meeting with you has confirmed my interest in a position in management with A Big Financial. I look forward to hearing from you soon.

Sincerely,

Marshall Dillon

EXERCISE 51

Write Your Own Thank You or Follow-Up Letter

PURPOSE:

To write a follow-up letter to be sent after an interview.

INSTRUCTIONS:

Write a thank you letter to the person who conducted your job interview. Make it sincere and personal. Be sure that you restate why you are qualified for the specific job you seek. Refer to pages 119, 120 and 124 for help.

Use the space below to write the first draft.

APPENDIX I

Action Words

Accelerated	Delivered	Instructed	Raised
Accomplished	Demonstrated	Interpreted	Realized
Achieved	Designed	Interviewed	Received
Activated	Detected	Invented	Recommended
Adapted	Determined	Investigated	Reconciled
Adjusted	Developed	Launched	Recorded
Administered	Devised	Learned	Reduced
Adopted	Diagnosed	Lectured	Reevaluated
Advanced	Directed	Led	Referred
Advised	Discovered	Logged	Reinforced
Analyzed	Dispensed	Maintained	Reorganized
Applied	Disproved	Managed	Reported
Approved	Distributed	Mediated	Represented
Arbitrated	Drew Up	Molded	Researched
Arranged	Edited	Monitored	Resolved
Assembled	Effected	Motivated	Restored
Assisted	Eliminated	Navigated	Revamped
Attained	Encouraged	Negotiated	Reviewed
Audited	Enlarged	Obtained	Revised
Built	Enlisted	Operated	Routed
Calculated	Established	Ordered	Scheduled
Chaired	Estimated	Organized	Selected
Collected	Evaluated	Originated	Served
Communicated	Examined	Oversaw	Set Up
Compared	Executed	Participated	Sold
Completed	Expanded	Perceived	Solved
Composed	Expedited	Performed	Stimulated
Conceived	Financed	Persuaded	Streamlined
Conducted	Forecasted	Photographed	Strengthened
Consolidated	Formulated	Pinpointed	Structured
Constructed	Founded	Planned	Studied
Consulted	Generated	Predicted	Succeeded
Contributed	Guided	Prepared	Suggested
Controlled	Hired	Presented	Summarized
Convinced	Implemented	Produced	Supplied
Coordinated	Improved	Programmed	Supported
Corresponded	Increased	Projected	Systematized
Counseled	Influenced	Promoted	Taught
Created	Informed	Proposed	Tested
Dealt	Initiated	Protected	Trained
Dealt With	Inspected	Proved	Translated
Defined	Installed	Provided	Updated
Delegated	Instituted	Purchased	Wrote

APPENDIX II

Descriptive Words

Accurately	Energetic	Persistent
Active	Enriching	Personable
Acuity	Enterprising	Pioneering
Adaptable	Enthusiastic	Pleasant
Adept	Exceptional	Positive
Alert	Exceptionally Broad	Productive
Ambitious	Expert	Proficient
Analytical	Extensively	Punctual
Artful	Extroverted	Quick
Assertive	Fair	Quickly
Astute	Firm	Readily
Attentive	Forceful	Realistic
Attractive	Helpful	Reliability
Aware	High-level	Reliable
Bright	Highest	Repeatedly
Broad	Highly	Resourceful
Broad-based	Honest	Responsible
Broad-minded	Honestly	Responsive
Calm	Humanizing	Self-reliant
Caring	Humorous	Sense of Urgency
Challenging	Imaginative	Sense of Humor
Competent	Increasingly Able	Sensitive
Conscientious	Independent	Significant
Consistent	Initiative	Significantly
Constructive	Innovative	Sincere
Contagious	Instrumental	Sophisticated
Contributed greatly	Kind	Stimulating
Courageous	Lead	Strong
Creative	Leading	Strongly
Deep Insight	Lifelong	Successful
Deft	Logical	Sympathetic
Dependability	Loyal	Systematic
Dependable	Mastery	Tactful
Determined	Mature	Talented
Diplomatic	Methodical	Think on Feet
Diplomatically	Natural	Thoughtful
Disciplined	Never Forgets	Trained
Discrete	New and Improved	Uncommon
Discretion	Objective	Unique
Diverse	Objectivity	Unusual
Drive	Open-minded	Unusual Grasp
Dynamic	Optimistic	Urgently
Earning Respect	Outgoing	Versatile
Economical	Outstanding	Vigorous
Efficient	Perceptive	Well-balanced
Efficiently	Perceivable	Well-rounded

APPENDIX III

Skills List

Accounting Skills
Acting Skills
Administration Skills
Analyzing Skills
Artistic Skills
Athletic Skills
Bargaining Skills
Bookkeeping Skills
Budget Planning Skills
Coaching Skills
Communications Skills
Computing Skills
Consulting Skills
Coordination Skills
Counseling Skills
Creative Skills
Culinary Skills
Debating Skills
Decision-making Skills
Designing Skills
Detail/Follow-through Skills
Driving Skills
Editing Skills
Evaluating Skills
Executing Skills
Farming Skills
Filing Skills
Financial-planning Skills
Fundraising Skills
Goal-setting Skills
Group Leadership Skills
Horticultural Skills
Human Relations Skills
Innovating Skills
Interpersonal Communication Skills
Interpreting Skills
Interviewing Skills
Landscaping Skills
Language Skills
Leadership Skills
Listening Skills
Machine Skills
Management Skills
Manual Skills
Marketing Skills
Math Skills
Memory Skills
Merchandising Skills
Money Management Skills
Motivational Skills
Musical Skills
Navigating Skills
Negotiating Skills
Nursing Skills
Observational Skills
Organizational Skills
Outdoor Survival Skills
Performing Skills
Personal Selling Skills
Persuading Skills
Planning Skills
Presentation Skills
Problem-solving Skills
Public-speaking Skills
Reading Skills
Record-keeping Skills
Researching Skills
Selling Skills
Supervisory Skills
Teaching Skills
Time Management Skills
Troubleshooting Skills
Training and Development Skills
Writing Skills

APPENDIX IV

Two-Letter State and Territory Abbreviations

Alabama	AL	Nebraska	NE
Alaska	AK	Nevada	NV
Arizona	AZ	New Hampshire	NH
Arkansas	AR	New Jersey	NJ
American Samoa	AS	New Mexico	NM
California	CA	New York	NY
Colorado	CO	North Carolina	NC
Connecticut	CT	North Dakota	ND
Delaware	DE	Northern Mariana Is.	CM
District of Columbia	DC	Ohio	OH
Florida	FL	Oklahoma	OK
Georgia	GA	Oregon	OR
Hawaii	HI	Pennsylvania	PA
Idaho	ID	Puerto Rico	PR
Illinois	IL	Rhode Island	RI
Indiana	IN	South Carolina	SC
Iowa	IA	South Dakota	SD
Kansas	KS	Tennessee	TN
Kentucky	KY	Trust Territory	TT
Louisiana	LA	Texas	TX
Maine	ME	Utah	UT
Maryland	MD	Vermont	VT
Massachusetts	MA	Virginia	VA
Michigan	MI	Virgin Islands	VI
Minnesota	MN	Washington	WA
Mississippi	MS	West Virginia	WV
Missouri	MO	Wisconsin	WI
Montana	MT	Wyoming	WY

APPENDIX V

Sources of Information about Careers, Job Listings, and Potential Employers

Career Employment Opportunities Directory--Liberal Arts and Social Sciences

Directory Information Services Supplement. James M. Ethridge, ed.

Directory of Corporate Affiliations. National Register Publishing Company

Directories in Print: An Annotated Guide to Business and Industrial Directories, Professional and Scientific Rosters, and Other Lists and Guides of All Kinds. Gale Research Co.

Directory of Industry Data Sources: The United States of America and Canada. Harfax, Ballinger Publishing Company, Paul Wasserman, ed.

Encyclopedia of Business Information Sources. Paul Wasserman, ed.

Executive Employment Guide. American Management Association.

Guide to American Directories. Bernard Klein.

How to Find Information about Companies. Washington Researchers.

Million Dollar Directory. Dun and Bradstreet, Inc.

National Business Employment Weekly.

National Directory of Addresses and Telephone Numbers. Kristin S. Loomis et al., eds.

National Health Directory. John T. Gruppenhorf, ed.

Nelson's National Directory of Wall Street Research. Nelson Productions.

Patterson's American Education.

Patterson's Guide to Careers and Employment: Physical Science, Computer Science and Engineering.

Standard and Poor's Register of Corporations, Directors, and Executives. Standard and Poor Corporation.

The Career Guide: Dun's Employment Opportunities Directory. Dun and Bradstreet Corp.

The Federal Yellow Book Directory. Washington Monitor. Quarterly.

The New York Times.

The Prentice-Hall Directory of Executive Search Firms.

Wall Street Journal.

Ward's Directory of 55,000 Largest U.S. Corporations. Information Access Corp.

ASHLEY ELIZABETH EUBANKS

1408 NW 19th Street
Gainesville, Florida 32605
(904) 555-0014

OBJECTIVE

An entry-level position in retail sales management.

EDUCATION

BEST JUNIOR COLLEGE, Gainesville, Florida
Associates of Arts: Liberal Arts, May 19XX

ACTIVITIES

Marketing Club: Assistant Social Chairman, 19XX-19XX
Developed organizational and budget planning skills while coordinating socials and seminars.

Best Junior College French Club, 19XX-present
Participated in weekly meetings to further international communications skills.

EXPERIENCE

Customer Service Representative, Applewood, Ocala, FL   19xx-present
Manage transaction and use accounting skills to compute daily revenue reports for a gift shop. Gained extensive knowledge of public relations skills with both co-workers and customers. Applied product knowledge and designing skills while creating seasonal displays.

Cashier/Waitress/Caterer, Fondu-Loch, Waldo, FL   19xx-19xx
Developed culinary skills in catering while working in conjunction with owner in preparation and execution of events including receptions, business functions, and private parties. Trained new employees.

OTHER DATA

Working knowledge of BASIC.
Highly Developed skills in customer relations.
Proficiency in French.
Extensive travel throughout Europe while living in West Germany.
Hobbies include piano, ballet, and water-skiing.

REFERENCES AVAILABLE UPON REQUEST

JOSEPH DRURY

Present Address:
P.O. Box 216
Atlanta, GA 30302
(404) 555-8678

Present Address:
P.O. Box 4323
Teeville, NC 28681
(704) 555-9800

OBJECTIVE: Veterinarian assistant or technician position.

EDUCATION: **Top University**, Atlanta, GA, BS Candidate December, 19xx.
<u>Major:</u> Biology (Pre-medicine)
<u>Honors:</u> Dean's List
<u>Activities:</u> Volunteer Top University Participant

Top University, Charlotte, NC 19xx--19xx.
<u>Honors:</u> Letter of Commendation
<u>Activities:</u> Volunteer at Research and Rehabilitation of Raptors

EXPERIENCE: **Surgical Emergency Technician**, Mercy Memorial Hospital
Atlanta, GA 19xx--Present. Assist MD's, Residents, RN's & NA's in all aspects of emergency and critical care medicine. Learned sterile procedures.

Veterinary Technician, Valley Animal Hospital
Lilburn, GA 19xx--19xx. Performed diagnostic laboratory duties. Assisted veterinarians in all facets of animal care.

Veterinary Technician, Central Animal Emergency Clinic
Homeville, GA 19xx–19xx. Performed veterinary assistance in emergency setting. Became competent in diagnostic tests, X-ray administration, surgical assistance, and autoclaving.

Property Manager, Franklin Park, Atlanta, GA 19xx -1 9xx.
Coordinated all aspects of apartment complex management. Became proficient in dealing with the general public.

Electronics Laboratorian, Milo's Dairy Corporation
Franklin-Glen, NY 19xx--19xx. Performed all electronic repair work at two production plant locations. Proved efficiency in working unsupervised.

Military, USMC, 19xx--19xx.
<u>Honors:</u> Meritoriously promoted. Received Honorable Discharge.

ADDITIONAL DATA: Recipient of two New York State Regents Scholarships.
Earned 100% of college expenses through GI Bill, employment, and loans.
Volunteer service at St. Bernard's Catholic Church, Atlanta, GA.
Volunteer at Mercy's Labor & Delivery Unit.
Workable knowledge of BASIC computer language.

REFERENCES: Available upon request.

SARAH MELONY GRIFFIN

205 Glendale Ave., Apt. A2
Boston, MA 02215

Home: (617) 555-0923
Office: (617) 555-6931

OBJECTIVE

To obtain a position as a Management Trainee.

SUMMARY

Responsible professional with management experience, excellent organizational, interpersonal, and time management skills. Promoted to supervisory level within one year of employment. Appointed Acting Department Head, 19xx. Possess variety of technical skills in desktop publishing, video, and audio.

PROFESSIONAL EXPERIENCE

TOP UNIVERSITY, Boston, MA   Sept. 19xx--Present
Media Services Supervisor

- Manage department providing support services to over 40 university departments.
- Consult with customers to assess audiovisual needs.
- Hire, train, supervise and evaluate staff.
- Establish and maintain departmental equipment inventory.
- Organize budget information for administrators.
- Direct work of staff on daily basis.
- Formulate and implement departmental policies.

Production Center Assistant   Oct. 19xx--Sept. 19xx

- Advised customers in graphic design and equipment use for presentations.
- Created graphics, posters, and publicity handouts for university events.
- Managed Production Center operations in the absence of supervisor.
- Received and accounted for cash, checks, and departmental accounts.
- Prepared monthly billing and statistics.

ADDITIONAL TRAINING

- Association for Educational Communications and Technology Annual Conference workshops, New Orleans, 19xx, and Atlanta, 19xx.
- Supervisory Training Program, Top University, 19xx.
- Seminar: "How to Manage People," Boston, 19xx.

MEMBERSHIPS

- *Association for Educational Communications and Technology.*
- *DOBIS Publicity Committee*, Top University.
- *Media Co-op*, Top University.
- *Broadband Task Force*, Top University.

EDUCATION

Bachelor of Arts, 19xx
Double Major

Top University, New Jersey
Communication and Journalism

JEFFREY P. WILLIAMS

Present Address:
312 Highland Road
Ithaca, NY 19504
(615) 555-8851

Permanent Address:
13548 Engel Drive
Brookfield, WI 53005
(414) 555-1273

PROFILE Ambitious, reliable individual with a dynamic and versatile background seeks a position using human relations skills in marketing or management.

EDUCATION **TOP UNIVERSITY**, Ithaca, NY, May 19XX
Bachelor of Arts, Philosophy
GPA: 3.5/4.0 Dean's List

BRITISH UNIVERSITY, London, England. Fall 19XX. GPA: 3.5/4.0. Excelled in Accounting, Geographical Perspectives of Modern Society, and Population, Economy, and Society courses. Obtained general knowledge of multi-national customs, cultures, and business practices. Interacted with students from all over the world. Traveled extensively throughout Great Britain and Europe.

ACTIVITIES Philosophy Honor Society--Phi Sigma Tau.
Benjamin S. Pius Pre-Law Society.
Intramural Basketball, Football, and Softball.
Top University Basketball Team.
British School of Economics Rugby Team.

EXPERIENCE **LEGISLATIVE INTERN**
Administrative Office of the Courts, Best Town, NY. 19XX.
Worked closely with Assistant Director. Tracked legislation affecting state court system. Attended House and Senate sessions and committee meetings. Conducted legislative research. Developed data entry, record keeping, and general office skills.

CREW CHIEF
Park and Recreation Department, Brookfield, WI. Summers, 19XX-19XX.
Responsibilities included working closely with Park and Recreation Supervisors. Supervised and trained various new employees. Maintained park facilities. Responsible for obtaining overtime pay for the seasonal employees.

ADDITIONAL INFORMATION Enjoy helping handicapped children.
Special interest in international relations.
Excelled in Business Communications course.

REFERENCES Available upon request.

KEVIN E. SANDERS
P.O. Box 25725
Honolulu, Hawaii 90322
(808) 555-5898

OBJECTIVE — A position as a flight attendant with a service oriented airline, where previous experience in travel and in dealing with the public can be used.

EDUCATION — **Top University, School of Business**
Honolulu, Hawaii.
BBA in Accounting: August 19XX

Intraskills, Inc. Courses
Orlando, Florida.
Effective Speaking and Human Relations
100% Competition Award: August 19XX

EXPERIENCE — **Travel Consultant**
Kiwi Travel Management, Honolulu, Hawaii
Confirmed reservations for corporate clients using DATAS II computer reservations system. Worked in the company's three branches. Developed the ability to work as a team member.
January 19XX--present

Graduate Assistant
Intraskills, Inc. Courses, Orlando, Florida
Participated as a member of the instructional staff. Kept records of class member participation and gave example talks as instructional tools. Became a better leader and developed listening skills.
January 19XX- December 19XX

Senior Travel Consultant
Business Executive Travel, Honolulu, Hawaii
Confirmed reservations, edited company newsletter, and prepared weekly ARC sales reports. Trained new agents on the use of DATAS II, company policies, and in-house accounting procedures. Learned to deal effectively with customers by using tact and authority.
March 19XX- December 19XX

SPECIAL SKILLS — Proficient in German
Licensed Private Pilot
Highly trained in DATAS II
Certified lifeguard
Fluent in airline and city codes

INTERESTS — Physical fitness, racquetball, snow skiing, travel, public speaking

REFERENCES — Provided upon request

JEANNE MARIE KING
420 Heather Road
Gettysburg, PA 17428
(717) 555-9003

SUMMARY

A goal-oriented elementary education teacher, using highly motivational techniques to provide structure, direction, and approval to individual needs in skills development.

TEACHING EXPERIENCE

Havasmile School, Lancaster, PA, September 19xx--present.
Teach kindergarten and four-year-old nursery school children.

Yellow Duck Day Care, Dover, PA, April 19xx - August 19xx.
Reading tutor and director of arts and crafts.

TEACHING ACCOMPLISHMENTS

Organized and developed the Havasmile Kindergarten program.

Designed a reading program combining the Beka curriculum, personal resources, and teaching ideas from articles, presentations, and other curricula.

Organized and structured math, science, and language development programs.

Developed a series of learning centers and bulletin boards that correspond with math, science, and reading units.

Established and cultivated excellent rapport with parents.

EDUCATIONAL RECORD

Bachelor of Science in Elementary Education with a cognitive area in Reading, December, 19xx.
Best College, York, PA.

Associate of Science in Liberal Arts, May, 19xx.
Best College, York, PA.

CERTIFICATION

Instructional I Elementary Education.
State of Pennsylvania.

REFERENCES

Available upon request.

AMY L. WATSON
144 Southlawn Avenue
Riverside, CA 92521
(714) 555-0375

PROFILE: Creative, organized individual seeks a challenging and growth-oriented position in marketing. Special interests: advertising and promotion.

EDUCATION: Top University, Riverside, CA 19XX
A.B.J. degree: Advertising
G.P.A. 3.2/4.0
Dean's List
Advertising Club
Additional coursework in marketing and management.

EXPERIENCE: *Pledge Coordinator*
Donor's Counsel, Inc., November 19XX-present.
- Review and sort prospect forms for 18 separate college fundraising campaigns.
- Categorize contracts according to particular campaign and special requests.
- Coordinate the efforts and accomplishments of fundraising callers with respect to follow-up paperwork.
- Teach proper research procedure to fundraising callers.
- Indicate specific campaigns that require special attention.
- Monitor prospect forms and corresponding paperwork for accuracy in preparation for data entry.

Advertising Intern
TOP/ADS, Inc., Media Department,
September-December 19XX.
- Performed data entry of radio and television schedules on Donovan Data System.
- Participated in research on a minority media plan for Sun Air Lines.
- Assisted with newspaper lineage analysis of group vs. individual contracts.
- Researched rates for periodicals and special event programs.
- Notified media of cancellations for national accounts.
- Became familiar with Lotus 1-2-3 software package.

OTHER DATA: Served as High School Reunion Chairman. Planned, coordinated, and implemented a 5-year class reunion for 300 people.
Working knowledge of Spanish language.
Extensive travel in United States, Canada, Mexico, and Europe.
Interests include reading, aerobics, soccer, and classical piano.

REFERENCES FURNISHED UPON REQUEST

JON A. LEVINE

PRESENT ADDRESS:
315 Walnut Drive
Las Cruces, NM 30317
(505) 555-3342

PERMANENT ADDRESS:
83 St. Charles Avenue
Cambridge, CT 04700
(302) 555-5693

OBJECTIVE: A position in a financial management training program.

EDUCATION: **TOP UNIVERSITY,**
School of Business Administration, Las Cruces, NM.
Candidate for BBA, Finance; May 19xx.
Cum. GPA: 3.78/4.0 Dean's List: Fall 19xx--present.

ACTIVITIES: Reform Jewish Students Committee, Vice President 19xx-19xx, Executive Secretary 19xx-19xx; University Center Board Special Events Committee, Chairperson, 19xx; Ad Hoc, musical theater group.

EXPERIENCE: **FINANCIAL ANALYST**
American Family Life Insurance Company,
Jordan, PA. June 19xx--present.

ACCOMPLISHMENTS: Prepared Company Expense Budget and Forecast. Drew up Cost Analyses. Conducted Strategic and Competitor Research. Revised Investment Committee Report.
RESPONSIBILITIES: Financial and Investment Analysis and Reporting.

ASSISTANT TO FINANCIAL CONSULTANT
Money Services, Inc., Las Cruces, NM. May 19xx--December 19xx.

ACCOMPLISHMENTS: Compiled and reviewed data on investment securities. Assisted in management of investment portfolios. Prepared financial plans. Operated internal research systems.
RESPONSIBILITIES: Created and maintained client profit and loss worksheets, cash flow and portfolio analyses.

ADMINISTRATIVE OPERATIONS ANALYST
USA Information Systems, Morristown, NJ. May 19xx--August 19xx.

ACCOMPLISHMENTS: Organized inventory control system. Prepared budget analysis. Revised project expense tracking procedures. Improved employee time reporting procedure. Developed computer graphics presentations.
RESPONSIBILITIES: Development and implementation of administrative procedures.

ADDITIONAL DATA: **COMPUTER KNOWLEDGE:**
Micro: IBM, Apple. Software: Spreadsheet (Lotus 1-2-3), Word Processing, Graphics
Mainframe: FORTRAN, BASIC, Informix Database.
INTEREST:
Piano, Musical Theatre, Horseback Riding, and Racquetball.

IRENE M. NEELY

COLLEGE ADDRESS: P.O. Box 11550 Washington, DC 20057 (202) 555-1673	**HOME ADDRESS:** 2684 Oak Lawn Stony Brook, NY 11782 (516) 555-0873

PROFILE   Reliable, enthusiastic individual seeks position in a federal government agency.

EDUCATION   **TOP UNIVERSITY**, School of Government and Business Administration, Washington, DC. Candidate for BBA, International Marketing, May 19xx.

BEST COLLEGE, Ithaca, New York.
Full-time student from August 19xx-December 19xx.
ACTIVITIES: Volunteer: Adopt-a-Grandparent Program; Student Administration Association member; Turman Seminar Series.

EXPERIENCE   **GREAT FOOD SERVICE REPRESENTATIVE**
The Gatehouse, Princeton, NJ, August 19xx-Present.
ACCOMPLISHMENTS: Increased customer base with special promotions.
RESPONSIBILITIES: Greet all customers. Describe the products carried in order to promote food sales. Maintain cleanliness of the restaurant. Report daily figures directly to manager.

ASSISTANT MANAGER
Drake's Construction, Setauket, NY, Summer of 19xx.
ACCOMPLISHMENTS: Participated in establishing the business. Pinpointed appropriate name to be used by the business. Promoted managers' diverse abilities in order to gain a larger clientele.
RESPONSIBILITIES: Scheduled appointments. Ordered materials for all large jobs. Handled customer complaints. Monitored specific details of jobs that had been completed.

ASSISTANT OFFICE MANAGER
Expert Engineering, Smithtown, NY, January 19xx-May 19xx.
ACCOMPLISHMENTS: Provided general assistance to any clients in need of computer information.
RESPONSIBILITIES: Used computers to design mailings. Reorganized engineering manuals every 3 months. Delivered computers to various companies. Screened all calls to the office.

SALES ASSOCIATE
Bixby's Shoppers World, Patchogue, NY, Summer of 19xx.
ACCOMPLISHMENTS: Motivated co-workers to take pride in their work. Improved the atmosphere of the Men's Department through team work.
RESPONSIBILITIES: Operated computerized cash register. Opened and closed Men's Department 3 days each week. Recorded daily sales. Delegated responsibilities to new employees.

INTERESTS   Working knowledge of BASIC computer language.
Enjoy tennis and jogging.

Academic and Professional References On Request.

CYNTHIA C. READING

2463 - Cherry Boulevard
Milwaukee, WI 53211
(414) 555-7141

OBJECTIVE: To obtain a position in Product Management.

EDUCATION: University of Wisconsin, Milwaukee, WI
Bachelor of Arts, May 19xx
Major: Art history; Concentration: Marketing
Grade Point Average in Major: 3.5/4.0

Activities: Student Admissions Association, Kappa Alpha Theta Sorority - Pledge Class Committee, Fraternity Education Committee, and Charity Work Volunteer, Sigma Chi Fraternity - Chapter Little Sister, Varsity Track Team, Field Hockey Club

SUMMER STUDY ABROAD, Paris/Arles, France May-June 19xx.
Emory University; Studied Roman, Romanesque and Modern Art.

WISCONSIN COLLEGE OF ART, Milwaukee, WI January-May 19xx.
Improved drawing skills through extensive project work.

EXPERIENCE: MANAGER OF ACCOUNTS PAYABLE: Monitor Group, Milwaukee, WI
Responsible for daily business transactions, including organizing invoices and paying bills. Duties included: Customer service, bookkeeping and filing. Attained quantitative skills in business management and improved skills in managerial communication. Summer 19xx.

ARCHITECT'S ASSISTANT: Wisconsin Trust for Historic Preservation, Milwaukee, WI. Researched historical buildings and drafted reconstruction plans. Evaluated color charts and selected potential facades. Photographed historical sites. Gained knowledge of historic preservation, architecture and building renovation. Improved communication skills, drafting and photography skills. Fall 19xx.

DATA PROCESSOR: General Press and Fabricating Co., Milwaukee, WI
Extensive use of Zenith H-90. Compiled customer lists and programmed computer for customer contact notices. Trained employees in computer data processing. Worked independently. Gained skills in time management and fluency with data processor. Summer 19xx.

ADVERTISING REPRESENTATIVE: Service Club, Milwaukee, WI
Increased account list and handled financing and follow-up of advertisement sales. Developed techniques in business persuasion and selling.
Summer 19xx.

ADMINISTRATIVE ASSISTANT: Monitor Group, Milwaukee, WI
Performed general secretarial duties and gained experience in small business management. Summers 19xx-19xx.

ADDITIONAL DATA: Extensive travel in U.S.A. and abroad. Working knowledge of French. Interests include traveling, painting, drawing, jogging and swimming.

REFERENCES: Available upon request.

Gregory D. Brown

Present Address
2743 Seton No. 216
Austin, TX 78705
(512) 555-6422

Permanent Address
200 Chestnut Drive
Wayne, NJ 07982
(201) 555-0901

Job Objective: A full-time position in sales with a future in sales management.

Education: **Top University**, Austin, TX. Bachelor of Arts with major in Economics. Graduation: June 19xx.

Rush Chairman of Omega Upsilon Delta Fraternity. Served as primary spokesperson while motivating the participation of over 100 members. Improved leadership potential by planning, coordinating, and supervising events such as Rush workshops, presentations, and initial membership selection for largest fraternity on campus. 19xx-19xx.

Job Experience:

Sales Representative. B&E Advertising-Austin, Texas. Determined price structures, marketed advertising space, and handled accounts receivable. Spring 19xx.

Sales Representative. Superior Advertising-Austin, Texas. Developed business skills by managing inventory, performing accounting duties, and directly marketing products. Trained, motivated and supervised new employees. Top salesman. Summer 19xx.

Assistant Manager. Short Hills Shoe Company, Short Hills, Texas. Improved customer relations ability by coordinating sales for business clothing and apparel store. Directed store operations in owner's absence. Winter 19xx.

Professional Experience: **Professional Vocalist/Musician**-Austin, Texas. Further developed projection and performance skills by performing for local clubs and bars. Spring 19xx.

Additional Data: **Volunteer** at State Psychiatric Hospital-Watchung, New Jersey. Ensured daily hygiene, comfort, and care for ten patients. Summer 19xx.
Working knowledge of BASIC computer language.
Working knowledge of Spanish.
Interests: Music composition, sailing, camping, and snorkeling.

References: Furnished upon request.

JONATHAN BRIAN WARNER

PRESENT ADDRESS: 10-C Buford Highway Atlanta, GA 30329 (404) 555-9046	**PERMANENT ADDRESS:** 1323 Crosby Drive Allentown, PA 19034 (215) 555-1142

OBJECTIVE: A position in the field of international corporate law.

EDUCATION: **TOP UNIVERSITY**, Atlanta, GA.
Candidate for Bachelor of Arts, History/Romance Languages, May, 19xx. Cumulative GPA: 3.7/4.0

BEST COLLEGE, Atlanta, GA.
Special studies in the Japanese language, customs and culture. Academic year, 19xx - 19xx. Cumulative GPA: 4.0/4.0

HONORS AND ACTIVITIES:
DEAN'S LIST
PHI SIGMA IOTA, National Foreign Language Honor Society.
OUTSTANDING PERFORMANCE IN FRENCH, 19xx.
RESIDENCE ASSOCIATION SPORTS DIRECTOR, 19xx.
AIESEC, present.
SPORTS STAFF WRITER, *Top Mirror*, present.

EXPERIENCE: **LOCAL SPORTS COLUMNIST**
Flannelly Publishing, Inc., Ft. Washington, PA. Summers, 19xx, 19xx, 19xx. Served as staff sportswriter with weekly byline to the Greater Norristown Upper Montco American Legion baseball league for *The Tattler* and *Today's News*, local newspapers with a combined circulation of 75,000.

SPORTS CHAIRMAN, ALPHA EPSILON PI FRATERNITY
Academic years 19xx - 19xx and 19xx - 19xx. Member of the Executive Board of Alpha Epsilon Pi. Directed the fraternity sports program and coordinated fraternity sporting events. Worked closely with members of Top University Interfraternity Council, formulating and supervising university sports policies.

INTERPRETER AND DOCUMENT TRANSLATOR
Comilansa S.A. Corporation, Quito, Ecuador. December 19xx - June 19xx. Accompanied investors to Ecuador and observed business negotiations between company representatives and high-level officials of the Ecuadorian government. Met with and served as liaison between investors and the First Lady, the Vice-President and the Secretary of State of Ecuador.

ADDITIONAL DATA: Hobbies include soccer, tennis, sportswriting and languages. Extensive travel in Spain, the Carribean and the U.S. Proficient in Spanish; working knowledge of Japanese.

REFERENCES: Furnished upon request.

Sheila M. Murphy

3709 Janice Drive
West Chester, Ohio 45069
(513) 555-9507

OBJECTIVE: Seeking a position where experience and skills with magnetic resonance imaging can be used and broadened.

EXPERIENCE: *Magnetic Resonance Imaging Technologist*
Top University, School of Medicine
Operate Philips Gyroscan 0.5 and 1.5 Tesla systems
Photograph using MI-10 Laser Camera
Developed teaching and organization skills by training student technologists
June 19xx-Present

Computerized Tomography Technologist
Top University, School of Medicine
Operated GE 1800 and Siemens Somatom Scanners
May 19xx-June 19xx

Radiologic Technologist
County Medical Center, Jupiter, ME
Performed routine diagnostic X-rays including fluoroscopy, angiography, OR and ER
November 19xx-April 19xx

EDUCATION: *Top University, School of Medicine*
Cincinnati, Ohio
Candidate for Bachelor of Medical Science in 19xx; Specialty in Teaching Radiologic Technologists
September 19xx-Present

Top University School of Medicine
Cincinnati, Ohio
Associate of Applied Science in Radiologic Technology
September 19xx

PROFESSIONAL CERTIFICATION: American Registry of Radiologic Technologists (ARRT)
October 19xx

PROFESSIONAL SOCIETIES: American Society of Radiologic Technologists (ASRT)
November 19xx-Present

REFERENCES: Furnished upon request.

MIGUEL TORRES-RODRIGUEZ

SCHOOL ADDRESS   **HOME ADDRESS**
P.O. Box 3960   P.O. Box 7349
Top University   Guayaquil-Ecuador
Fort Collins, CO 80523   South America
(303) 555-4591   (015934) 555-198

JOB OBJECTIVE A sales management training position that offers opportunities for a future career in the hospitality industry.

EDUCATION *TOP UNIVERSITY, Fort Collins, Colorado*
Candidate for Bachelor of Business Administration with a major in Management. December 19XX.

BEST COLLEGE, Denver, Colorado
Graduated with an AA in Liberal Arts, Fall 19XX. GPA 3.25/4.0. Honor List.

ECUADORIAN-GERMAN CULTURAL CENTER, Guayaquil, Ecuador.
Graduated with major in German, December 19XX.

EUROPA KOLLEG, Kassel, Germany
Received degree in the study of the German language. High Honor, May 19XX.

BENEDICT SCHOOL OF LANGUAGES, Guayaquil, Ecuador
Received degree in the English language, May 19XX.

TOP UNIVERSITY, Detroit, Michigan
Attended two English courses April 19XX.

EXPERIENCE *SALESMAN, L.E.L. Corporation, Guayaquil, Ecuador.*
Personally responsible for selling an expensive line of electrical equipment throughout the country.

SALES MANAGER ASSISTANT, L.E.L. Corporation, Guayaquil, Ecuador.
Supervised the Sales Department.

OTHER DATA Hobbies and interests include soccer, tennis, and waterskiing. Basic knowledge of BASIC, FORTRAN, and MINITAB computer languages. Traveled Europe, North and South America. Fluent in Spanish, English, and German with a basic knowledge of Portuguese.

REFERENCES Available upon request.

GARY ROBINSON PRICE

Present Address
123 Eastland Drive
Corvallis, Oregon 97331

(503) 555-3054

Permanent Address
456 Hillside Avenue
Glen Ellyn, Illinois 60137

(312) 555-0998

OBJECTIVE   A challenging position in marketing using management and entrepreneurial skills.

EDUCATION   **Top University Business College**   Corvallis, OR
Candidate for MBA degree, May 19XX
Activities: American Marketing Association, Entrepreneurial Club, Graduate Business Association, Intramural Coordinator.

Best Collge   Ripon, WI
BA Degree in Economics, Minor in Mathematics, May 19XX
Honors: Graduated Cum Laude, Dean's List, Omicron Delta Epsilon: Economic Honor Society.
Activities: Ripon Cable Network TV-Sports Editor: Organized and was responsible for broadcasting sports events to the local community.Indoor Soccer Club-President: Coached and organized three 12-team tournaments.Adams Handicap Swim Program: Taught swimming to handicapped youth.

EXPERIENCE   **Painting Contractor   Summers, 19XX-19XX**
P&P Painting Co.   *Chicago, IL*
Founded and managed an interior/exterior residential and commercial painting business. Duties included bookkeeping, estimating, advertising, and payroll. Contributed capital investment for purchasing of supplies and equipment. Responsible for training and scheduling staff, controlling operating expenses, and customer relations. Helped finance more than 85% of educational expenses.

Special Projects Assistant   **Spring 19XX**
Downes, Gross & Peters Advertising   *Portland, OR*
Promoted the implementation of a new real estate listing service. Actively involved in research on and servicing of Red Machine account. Compiled market share data of 26 cities. Worked as a liaison between the Public Relations and Media Departments.

Athletic Field Maintenance Coord. Summers 19XX-19XX
Restful Park District   *Glen Ellyn, IL*
Supervised field maintenance. Exercised planning skills assigning groundskeeping responsibilities for softball and soccer fields.

ADDITIONAL DATA   Boy Scouts of America: Eagle Scout.
Working knowledge of BASIC, MINITAB, and Lotus 1-2-3.
Traveled extensively throughout Western Europe and the Continental United States. Enjoy racquet sports, snow and water skiing.

REFERENCES   Available upon request